Dementia can't take everything!

Bringing back moments that matter

Wendy Hall

First paperback edition March 2021

Book cover design by Daria DiCieli

ISBN 978-0-6451185-0-6 (paperback)

www.dementiadoulas.com.au

CONTENTS

Preface

When I was planning this book, I wondered how I would do it. I thought about how I could go about creating stories and share them in a way that would connect with and inspire others. It finally hit me that all the stories I wanted to write had already been written, the hard part had already been done. I realised that my job in all of this was to put them into print so that they could be shared. I needed to bring them to life in a way that others could better connect with them. I could see clearly that the stories that I've shared in for so many years were there waiting to be heard. They were waiting to be brought together as one so we can honour them and so that other people know that their own stories are just as important.

I unapologetically say that this book is a result of all the frustrations I've had bottled up inside me over the years. I know many colleagues and acquaintances along the way have also felt similar frustrations: the frustration of not seeing staff in dementia care being truly valued or their true skills optimised, frustration for those living with dementia who remained unseen, unheard, and left without a voice, frustration for the family members who painstakingly took on a role they had never wanted or even willingly signed up to do, a role they do with dedication, love, tears, and with no idea what they are supposed to be doing. How is that fair to anyone? And that, in a nutshell, is why I'm here and I'm hoping that's why you're here too.

Welcome to this first book in a series that will endeavour to view dementia care in a whole new light and bring everyone together in a way that hasn't been done before. It's my story, my view, and the uniqueness of that is what I bring. I mention that because there are many fantastic resources and publications that do exist out there and I want to acknowledge that this is not a replication. I will share my account, my experiences and what I've learnt with the hope I have to continue learning from the people who matter most – those living with dementia.

This first edition of *Dementia can't take everything* will be mostly about my perspective. It will be about the things that people living with dementia, their families and my colleagues have taught me over the years. My hope is that it represents my openness to listen and to learn from those affected most. I hope further editions will contain more of your stories, your learnings and where you pledge to make a difference in this field. Whether you're living with dementia or supporting someone with dementia, we are all responsible for becoming the true voices for those without one and I sincerely hope I can do my small part in providing a platform to bring those voices together.

So, while this starts as my story, the parts that are missing are the parts that you're yet to write and share. The future of this series is waiting on you. This series will be an opportunity to share in dementia care from a perspective we've not had the opportunity to come from before - from yours and mine, from ours. You are now on a road of self-discovery and together we're going to share in not only a lot of laughter but likely quite a few tears. We'll share a heap of highs and we'll also share the lows. We'll share our frustrations with a system that has forgotten to progress, a system that ultimately says it's all too hard, a system that says, let's just stick to the script.

This book is my way of contributing, in the best way I know how, to bringing forward a perspective that is a fair representation of those impacted by dementia. I want to do justice to the stories others have shared with me, not because they wanted attention, but because they needed a voice, a voice they wanted desperately to be heard by others, to be able to share with the world how destructive this disease is and how much it has taken away from them.

So, if not a single person reads this book, I'm totally OK with that, because my goal is to ensure that these stories, and the many more to come, don't stay trapped within me and I have been the only one to have benefitted and learnt from them. If I was to keep to myself the stories of those who were brave enough to trust and share them with me, then what have I truly learnt?

I see my job as being a voice for the people themselves, to help in restoring their identity, the one that was so cruelly taken away from them. I don't care about dementia, I don't want to be a voice for dementia, I want to be a voice for all those impacted by the challenges it brings. Looking into the future, we don't have to look very far to see there's still so much to be done. My hope is that moving forward, you will join me and others like me in making a true difference. I need to share in and include your experiences and your stories, those that have bought you hope, connection and direction, so that we can make a difference. Together we can put dementia back in its box where it belongs.

The stories are not mine to credit, they're stories that have been entrusted to me over many years and they're stories shared with me in many forms. They're stories that have been so important for my growth and development, but I've always known they were never intended just for me. I've assured many along the way that their trusted stories, those that they've shared with me from the heart, would never just remain with me. I vowed to many that their brave stories would be used to educate others as to how much we get things wrong, the things we sometimes get right and how we can learn from them and move forward. These deeply personal stories have resulted in a lot of laughter and many tears and they include many moments of despair. But those stories have a purpose, and that purpose is to teach us how to do things better, how to connect and how to make a difference that has a true impact.

So, although the stories are not my own, the perspective is, and it's this perspective that I share. I share how those stories touched my heart and soul, how they influenced me to want to do more in this space. I grew tired of prescriptive caring and I knew I wanted to give more. I knew that those who trusted in me needed more from me.

I can't change the past and all that we've got wrong, but luckily the future is still to be written. So, with you by my side, we can give it a pretty good go. The best part will be bringing together amazing individuals who care and are prepared to roll up their sleeves and say, 'Right, where do we start?' Some of you have already started to surface and connect and that makes me not only excited but it's continuing to fuel a passion to make a dent in the tumultuous world of dementia. Together, we'll give back some of what dementia has taken away. This is a book that I hope brings comfort, peace and inspires change for those that need it most.

You hold the key, you always did. Whether you work in the dementia care industry, support someone living with dementia or you're living with dementia yourself, we need your stories, the stories that bring hope and learning, so that we all can be guided in providing support in a better way, an ever-evolving way. We'll never get it 100% right but I hope by capturing some of the amazing things that are happening locally but not being utilised widely, we can support not only the person with dementia but all their supporters too. I don't have all the answers, I really wish I did. But what I do have is the ability to connect with you and others because it's you that hold a piece of the puzzle that others so desperately need to guide their practice in a way they could never have imagined.

If you're here purely for the read, that's great. You just became an ambassador for the cause and you now get to spread what you learn to your fellow staff, your local community, along with family and friends. You have the opportunity to reflect on how tomorrow you'll do it just that bit better than you did today. I'm excited and humbled to be purely the vessel through which your stories will join with others and make a difference in the future - support for people living with dementia and those standing by their side.

Over the years I have captured quotes that I have interwoven throughout the book. They are reminders to me and to all of us that we're working and supporting real people, and not only are they real people but diverse people; people from different backgrounds, different cultures, different countries, different religions, different communities, different neighborhoods, different families. We must never lose sight of the fact that we support individuals. A one size fits all approach is no longer going to serve us moving forward. In fact, it never really served us to start with. But we know more now and are finally starting to listen and not just becoming more proficient at telling. We are finally at the start of something new, something that we get to create, shape and make a difference. My greatest hope for you is that you decide today to get on board and come along for the ride.

My motivation for capturing quotes over the years was for two specific reasons. Firstly, to remind me that the effects of dementia go much wider than the clinical manifestation and secondly, to give me an idea as to where I needed to head next. Those quotes are from families, staff and those living everyday with dementia and they are clear expressions of what they need from us. In many instances, all we need to do is listen.

I lastly want to share with you the meaning of the cover of this book. My illustrator captured the obscure brief I gave her perfectly. While I personally feature in illustration form, this book is not my story, it's merely my perspective. The cover depicts stories being released and shared from a book so that others may better connect and understand. The book can also be seen drawing stories into it as well. The book has no cover and that's because the book you see me holding is yet to been written. It's the future version of the one you're currently reading and the one I hope you'll feel inspired to contribute to.

1 • Why should we bother?

'The more we know about the aspects and types of relationships that are meaningful and personally gratifying for all partners in care, the better able we will be to help nurture such relationships.'

- L. de Witt and D. Fortune, p. 1160

Historically we knew so little about dementia. For most of us, our learning over the last twenty to thirty years generally came straight from the pages of a biology textbook. We sort of gleaned an understanding of what was going on in the brain but never really learnt anything to tangibly help us understand the person's experience or how we could best support them. Many of us entered the world of dementia and learnt to just 'wing it' and might I say, during my time, I've seen some amazing things happening out there. But, unfortunately on the flipside and without any true guidance, I also saw things that saddened me to the core. I vowed to one day make some sort of tangible difference. I knew from the start it would be a big call, that I am but one person and I therefore put out the call for likeminded individuals just like you to join me.

What I do know, is that often people are drawn to work in this area due to the compassion they feel and the need to make a difference in the lives of others. So, our benchmark for so long has been working along the lines of what feels right to us, developing our own individual strategies and adapting them if things don't go to plan. But what has also happened, unfortunately, is that without a true guide and understanding of what's going on out there, many amazing colleagues have become disgruntled. They have felt devalued and unrecognised in an industry that still says, 'as long as you tick all the boxes then your job is done.' The 'touchy, feely' stuff that's so important to our practice has long been viewed as a nice to have rather than an absolute necessity of dementia care. It's the stuff that's not necessarily quantifiable but which at times matters more than anything to the person we are there to serve.

I remember about ten years ago moving into a new role that saw me moving away from directly working with those living with dementia and their families. As I moved into a more education-based role, I ran into a family member who voiced his disappointment that I had moved on and 'left them'. I felt in that moment a sense of sadness, as if I were abandoning him and his family, along with those that needed me most.

I thought for a moment and then said to him, 'I need to do this role, it's an opportunity for me to get in people's faces and share your stories, to make them listen so that they will be ready to better support all who will need their care. I won't stop telling your stories and I'll make people understand what life is like for you all. I'll let them know what you need from people like us.'

He smiled, nodded, and said, 'Good, I'm glad to hear.'

It's important that we don't give up on dementia, because when we do, when we feel defeated, we effectively give up on the person. Although that's what we've done historically, I don't know a single person who has done so willingly. This book is intended as a conversation starter, one that allows us, as support providers, to have a voice and to inspire others to share their stories; stories and lessons that create special and tangible moments to be acknowledged and valued without just letting them pass by. It's time to capture and share those moments so that tomorrow we can be just that bit better in what we do, and the day after we strive to be even better again because when times get tough, we, as support providers, will always have the option of packing up and going home. Those impacted by advancing dementia don't have that same choice. They just need to keep showing up day after day and going it alone. We all need that to change.

Have you ever had a dream where you feel like you're trying to communicate with people, and they can't hear you even though you desperately try to yell and scream? You try as hard as you can, but people just can't hear you. Then you wake from that dream and you may be in a cold sweat, you may be crying, you are physically shaken and thanking heaven on earth that it was just a dream, a nightmare that you got to wake up from. Imagine for a moment that you couldn't wake from that dream because it had become your reality, just like someone with advancing dementia who doesn't get to wake up from that reality. Imagine living each day and night where you try to reach out, you try to talk. If you find that you do have the ability to yell or scream it is then viewed as a symptom of a disease and is therefore something to be controlled or managed. Where do you go from there, when that scream was all that you had left to try to connect with the world around you?

Sharing the stage

This book will attempt to move the spotlight off dementia, the disease, and to put it back on the person where it belongs. I recall a session I delivered to care home staff around the experience of dementia for the person. I knew that staff would only be receptive to change if they could somehow feel the experience for themselves. As we commenced, a female resident joined the back of the group and asked if it was OK if she stayed. She was warmly welcomed and sat for the two-hour duration. While discussing communication and the challenges dementia creates, the woman slowly raised her hand and asked if she could say something. Her words were defining of the moment and summarised perfectly the messages I was trying to get across. She softly said, 'We can hear what you say but we don't always understand what you say.'

For that moment in time, Heather had an identity, and she had a voice, a voice that was heard by those that mattered most, those who would ultimately support her over the coming years. Thirty staff members were her captive audience and they listened to her with intent. In that moment, I knew they were touched by her words and her insight. Heather had shared a glimpse into her daily world, a world that staff walked through every day without a second thought about what it might be like to live there on a permanent basis.

I felt moved that I, in some small way, was able to create that moment for her, to effectively stop time so that she could say what she wanted others to see and feel. I saw the respect that staff showed Heather and the confidence this gave her to speak. She contributed something that would not only impact on her own care but also that of other residents. Heather stepped up and knew this was her moment. As she nervously spoke, she ended by apologising for interrupting and hoped that what she had said made sense. I knew her message had come across loud and clear and I wish we could have bottled that moment for others to share. I could see a better way forward and knew that I could not only share the stories and learnings from those living with dementia, but also create a stage from which they could speak for themselves.

There was one more gem still to come. Heather spoke with the care home manager following the session and said to her, 'It means so much to me that everyone (staff) would sit there for so long listening to what it's like for us.' As the manager recalled the conversation to me, we both stood looking at each other teary eyed. This was a moment neither of us would forget. I was fortunate to meet with Heather and thanked her for sharing her insights. I assured her that what she shared would have impacted staff in a way I could only ever hope to achieve.

Building the platform for change

Change in dementia care and culture can only come when those passionate and driven about a cause take those important steps to make it happen. In order to influence change, we first need to look at ourselves and identify the true role we play. If we are totally honest with ourselves, we may see something that doesn't sit comfortably with us or that we're not proud of. You may find yourself over time thinking things like, 'I wish I could spend more time with someone and do the added extras they need and deserve. I wish I had time to go and sit with the person who continues to call out.' If we don't truly identify our place in all of this then the battle is lost even before it's begun.

The thing is, there are a lot of mistakes that occur in this area but on the flipside there are a lot of amazing things that happen too. So, let's start with a frank conversation on service provision for someone living with advancing dementia and that's when true change will begin. I believe that you, as an individual, has what it takes to make a difference. Imagine if we said to ourselves, 'I think that I already do a good job in supporting those impacted by dementia – but could I do it even better?' When we ask this of ourselves, we are instantly open to new possibilities and a new way of thinking. That's when the magic can and will happen. There are others out there, just like Heather, waiting for the change that only you can bring.

While there are processes in place for everything to do with clinical care and personal care, how we tackle everything else is done in a much more ad hoc fashion. It's time to reframe our thinking in a way that brings about a process for all the other intangible aspects that formalised procedures don't include. We need to dive deep into the current industry culture and identify our place within it. We must first look at where we've come from, what has influenced our practice and attitudes and why it still has such a great impact on us today. We must then identify the meaning of dementia and try to frame it in a way that we can all better connect with.

The word 'dementia' continues to be such an ambiguous term and leaves everyone who uses it with a different image of what it actually means and who we think it impacts. We need to explore who the people living with dementia are so that we can move away from seeing them as a disease and instead for who they are at the core. We can do this by attempting to walk in their shoes, to try for a moment to see life from their perspective so that we better understand the people we are trying so desperately to connect with. To think about context and what it's like to live without it must undoubtedly play a part. Knowing what dementia is and how it impacts our everyday existence creates a solid foundation for moving forward. It will only be then that the answers we spend energy and frustration searching for are discovered closer and more obvious than we think.

Just imagine finding your true sense of purpose and developing your position into one of true fulfillment, one where your work becomes about fuelling your passion for making a difference. As I ventured along my own path of self-discovery, so many doors began opening for me. I found myself having conversations with people I least expected. My hope is that the same possibilities present themselves to you. You are such an important part of the puzzle and it's up to you to find exactly where you fit.

Working in dementia care

Dementia care would have to be one of the most complex areas to work in. It's an area where those working within in it receive very little formalised training which we know is required to develop and hone skills to meet the complexities this disease presents. We still know very little about the brain and what causes dementia. Most of the amazing work being done in this area continues to be done as a result of trial and error along with instinctive and intuitive practices by families and staff.

Imagine saying to a pilot or a surgeon, 'Here's your 6-week course on how to fly a plane or perform surgery. It's a very complicated area but I'm sure you'll be fine and pick up what you need along the way.' This just wouldn't happen because those receiving a specialised service expect someone to deliver, to have the skills and knowledge to do the best job possible. And it's a bonus if they can keep everyone safe along the way. Our lives are in their hands. Why, then, are the rules so different for those living with dementia? Don't they deserve the same level of professionalism and service? We know their lives should matter just as much, along with staff who deserve more so that they too can glean the same job satisfaction knowing their efforts are making a true difference.

Introducing self-reflection

To get things started, it's important to take a moment to reflect on where you are and where you truly fit into this area. Where do you think you're heading? Are you just curious about what current thinking is? Or are you here because you're ready to step up to the next level? It really doesn't matter, as long as you're honest with yourself as to where this all sits for you because when you are honest, that's when true change can happen.

We're so reliant on research and technology for our understanding of dementia and therefore limited in how fast our understanding can grow. While we continue to learn more, we need to remember to stay receptive to the 'lightbulb' moments that would normally just pass us by. These 'lightbulb' moments are not normally found in a textbook, but they can really impact on how we connect, regardless of whether the person is newly diagnosed or in the later stages of dementia.

Finding more than band-aid solutions

What I've found in the past is that when you open up the dialogue, what generally happens is that it brings up more questions than answers. I personally think that's a good thing. The answers are all out there, but it's up to us to get out there and find them. There's no tell all book, no lecture that will provide a quick fix solution. But by talking and sharing more, we'll find that there's often more than one answer or solution to the same question or issue. I never said this would be easy, but at least if we have more understanding at our disposal, we'll be more inclined to try different things and not give up so easily, especially after the first try.

Let's commit to thinking about dementia care a bit differently and to extend on the skills and knowledge that's already there. What we'll capture better moving forward are not the daily tasks, but the extra things that are done because someone thinks that's how they'd want someone to treat their mother or father. A lot of things that we as individuals contribute to the area of dementia are things that we just made up as we went along. A lot of the special extras are things that we weren't trained to do. This highlights that there are a lot of individuals out there who go unrecognised and are undervalued for the contributions that mean so much to those impacted by dementia.

I continue to find it inspiring when I see passionate staff constantly developing and redefining their unofficial skills as they go along. It's therefore my wish that by the time you finish reading this book you'll be thinking, 'Wait! Isn't there more? Where's the rest?' I look forward to the time when we finally wake up to the fact that we're a big part of the elusive and highly sought-after solution, and that moving forward it will be about coming together to influence the bigger picture, knowing that only then will change start to happen in a way we alone could never have imagined.

We won't be about changing the bigger and broader system; we'll be about getting the dialogue happening and letting the system catch up with us. We're going to open up the dialogue, you and I, and we'll do it in a way that we can better learn from each other. We can support and guide each other in the space of dementia care and hold our heads up high and say we gave it our best and we hope it makes a difference, however big or small.

We won't be about striving for monumental change and becoming bitter and twisted about the things we can't influence.

Let's focus on what we can change, the change that only you and I can bring, the 'us' and the true power we hold in making the life of someone living with dementia and their families better for today. You and I have no idea what's going to happen tomorrow. But you know what? Today, we've got this, and tomorrow we're going to make it happen.

Rosa's story …

If you never thought that you alone could make a difference, consider Rosa:

Rosa was a lady living in a residential care home. Staff had grown increasingly concerned because Rosa was throwing any food that was given to her straight at the window. This 'behaviour' was something they were having trouble 'fixing'. Staff would explain to Rosa that this was not acceptable, and she was often told off. Heated exchanges would follow, and staff continued to become concerned that they were unable to effectively 'manage' Rosa.

When working with the staff collectively, I asked what they knew about Rosa and the standard responses were given. They would offer suggestions such as gardening, cooking and family. While these were valuable insights, they lacked the depth required to fully understand what Rosa enjoyed about gardening, cooking or her family. For example, was it important to Rosa that she cooked for her family and not just cook in general?

After spending some time with staff and not making any real headway, I posed the following question to the group, 'What is one thing that you know about Rosa that you don't think anyone else here would know?' Staff gave some interesting feedback that included things she liked to eat and the music she liked to listen to, but then came the shift. A hand slowly rose from the back of the group and a quiet voice spoke. The male staff member looked uncomfortable at the prospect of speaking in front of the large group. He continued and said just a few powerful words. 'When Rosa throws food, she thinks she's feeding the birds.' We all stopped and paused for a moment. We had gone through some complex ideas of what might be going on for Rosa, but this was certainly not a path that had been previously explored.

When asked why he thought this was the case, he explained that on occasions he would take her outside and she loved feeding the birds. That one staff member held the key we were looking for but previously had neither the opportunity nor confidence to share this vital piece of information. Was it that Rosa just couldn't see the window in front of her? When staff knew the likely story, they responded and connected with Rosa in a totally different way and no further altercations occurred.

A few months later I was told that the manager of the unit had shared that on an occasion following this, he was walking through the common room and noticed Rosa throwing food at the window. He said that he had just stood there for a moment and smiled. He then walked over to Rosa and without saying a word adjusted her chair slightly, opened the sliding door so that the food could be thrown to the intended recipients. No medications or complex strategies were needed. One staff member: that's all it took to change the path that Rosa was headed along.

Question for reflection ...

Is the care you see in the area of dementia, the care you want waiting for you one day?

The gift ...

True change can only happen when we find the courage to look in the mirror and see the answer staring right back at us.

"I love what I do and the people I get to work with but I'm not sure if I can do this much longer ..."

* Care staff *

2 • Influences of past practices

*'Reliance on a solely medical framework has been
increasingly criticised for maintaining the exclusion and
passive dependency of people with dementia.'*

- T. Shakespeare, H. Zeilig & P. Mittler, p. 1078

Where have we come from?

Asking ourselves this question on a regular basis will
ultimately guide us in the direction we need to head. It will
enable us to begin pushing boundaries and question if we really
are contributing to best practice. In fairness, what we considered
best practice twenty years ago is in a lot of cases now
detrimental to someone living with dementia. That doesn't
mean we were bad people or didn't care, but it acknowledges
that we did what we did with the information we had at hand at
that specific moment in time. In so many areas we have grown
and developed, and this is reflected in the changes we have
started to make in the care we provide.

Dementia care has traditionally been a task focussed area. As Dr Atul Gawande tells us in his book 'Being Mortal', aged care has evolved under the direct influence of a hospital, nursing type model of care. As we know, the fast-paced hospital doesn't leave a lot of time available for self-reflection of practice, to be able to stand back and ask ourselves,' Did I do a good job?' or,' Did I make any mistakes today?' The hospital model of care is based on ticking boxes. A good shift is one where all the boxes were ticked. But what most people drawn to the areas of aged care and hospital care share is a common and genuine desire to make a positive difference to the lives of those they care for.

This certainly isn't an area you work in for the money. What is missing in the dementia setting is the opportunity to say, 'You know what? I stuffed up today.' We need to support each other with that because stuff ups are happening in dementia care every day and I challenge anyone to say they aren't. We are working with people who are often unable to tell us what their needs and wants are; so we spend a lot of our day guessing. And do you know what? I'm not a mind reader. I would be lucky to know what one person needs or wants, let alone the ten people I have been allocated. Just because you are starting to get a bit restless and it is midday, my likely starting point is that perhaps you're hungry. So when you throw the food I give you, I then say 'BEHAVIOUR, she's throwing her food.'

But it may be that just because it's lunchtime, food is not your actual need at this moment in time. Maybe all you need is to go to the toilet. I may or may not get it right but it's important that I'm not dismissive of the person's needs. Historically we've blamed behaviour on the disease. She threw the meal because she has dementia. All of this doesn't make me a bad person and I am going to tell you that I will keep trying to work out what it is that you do want. When I work it out, then I am going to document it so that it's a starting point for the next person.

Rather than get frustrated about it, I need to let you know that I'm going to keep trying. So, we're getting things wrong all the time in this area and we need to own that.

However, staff need to own the good things that happen as well, the wins, the triumphs the victories, big or small. It saddens me that time and time again I see so many good things happening out there and witness amazing staff not owning or connecting with them. Staff so often just choose to show up and do their best without a second thought of the role they actually play.

When the bar of expectation is set too high

Often the things that go wrong are the things that are not always obvious at the time. But 'getting it wrong' is often a case of not connecting the dots of who the person is and what the message is they may be trying to share. Past practices have seen us look at the person at face value and struggle to see past the veil of dementia.

I recall working with staff who were growing increasingly concerned and frightened of a resident, Sandra. Sandra would resist attempts at personal care and was becoming more verbally aggressive towards staff. As we explored who Sandra was as a person and how staff responded to her, a staff member said, 'She used to work here as the Matron and so she tries to act like she's still in charge. I tell her she isn't a nurse here anymore.' This was a moment to hit the pause button and go back to the beginning. Staff knew who Sandra had been in the past and who she now was. Unfortunately, dementia had not afforded Sandra that same courtesy. We needed to create a version of Sandra's experience that staff could see and connect with. Staff needed a better view of the world that Sandra was now living in. We reflected on how confronting it would be to find yourself, with dementia, confused but still aware of your familiar surroundings. Now imagine realising that those familiar surroundings are your place of work and you are still in your pyjamas with curlers in your hair. How frightening to then be told that you don't work there anymore by staff who no longer resemble the colleagues you once knew.

It was by exploring Sandra's perspective that staff were able to have their own lightbulb moments, to connect with Sandra's experience in a way they had not even for a moment considered before - that dementia doesn't just affect a person's memory, but also creates a disorientating confusion that is difficult and stressful to navigate.

It's more than just dementia

We have all contributed in some way to getting it wrong in the past, but today is a new day, a new opportunity to create a safe environment where we can challenge each other to put up our hands and say we get it wrong and do so on a daily basis. I think we all need to be a bit nicer to ourselves about that rather than say, 'No, everything was fine, I didn't do anything wrong, it was the person's fault.' Own it! That's how we learn and that's how we'll grow as a team and as individuals. When we can freely admit to this, we take a big step forward. Everyone is doing their absolute best with often limited feedback from the person.

When looking back at where we've come from, I want to share some common dialogue that continues to be used even to this day. When asking a question like, 'Why does Rob get so aggressive?' a common reply will be, 'Because he has dementia.' How about, 'Why is Anne not eating?' Reply, 'Because she has dementia.' Or 'Why is Beryl so teary?' You guessed it 'Because she has dementia.' These stock standard responses will often come with a big full stop at the end of them. When used as a stock standard answer, it gives us permission to not look any further for additional causes. We've found the answer and its dementia that's to blame. But is it? If we put a full stop after a response like this, we take away any chance of finding out the true cause. There's always more to the story and it takes more than a throw away response to find and work out what's going on for the person.

Let's look at what is commonly said when someone with dementia has a good day. Mrs Smith can be seen having a 'good day'. She is coming down the corridor humming and in a spirited voice says, 'Good morning dear.' If I was to ask staff why Mrs Smith is so happy, they are likely to provide one of the following in reply:

1. 'She's just a happy dementia, she's like it all the time.'
2. 'They must have changed her medications.'
3. 'Must be a full moon.'

These responses must stop. The more likely reason is that Mrs Smith is happy because of you. There are people around Mrs Smith on that particular day who are making her feel comfortable and included. Staff need to stop giving credit to dementia, to drugs or the full moon. Staff deserve the recognition for when things are going well and residents are happy. What a missed opportunity to validate a wonderful achievement with peers and staff!

Basic care needs

When we go back in time, and we don't need to go back too far, it's evident that previously we knew so little about dementia. Care provision was based on the premise that there was a duty to make sure people were fed, watered, kept clean, had a roof over their heads and were administered their prescribed medications daily. These were the boxes that needed to be ticked. Fast forward to now, and it's only in more recent times that we're beginning to understand that those living with dementia need so much more than that.

Part of our evolving understanding in this area was based on the societal views of the time. Our practice over the years suggested that the person with dementia could be best described as, 'the lights are on, but no one's home.' So many other derogatory terms also followed. People were referred to as crazy, mad, senile and demented. The confusing thing for us was that when we worked with these people first-hand, there appeared to be a contradiction. The people we were working with all seemed to know what was going on, even if they could only retain the memory of it for a moment or two. There was always a connection and you always knew for better or for worse where you stood with the person. These are the conflicting messages that staff over time have had to navigate. It has always been left up to the individual to try to make their own sense of what is actually going on for the person. We have evolved with so many conflicting ideas within our practice and so much that never really made sense. How much of this has truly changed with time?

What we didn't do well historically was to rely on medications to fix things that appeared to be broken. Antipsychotics such as Haloperidol were the go-to drug of choice. If someone appeared agitated or aggressive, we reached for the antipsychotics. It is unfortunate that for all the things we have taken away from those living with dementia, we've never managed to fully evolve away from this practice. Change in this area is finally coming and it's great that the conversation about non-pharmacological medical interventions is now happening and being taken more seriously. The old adage of, 'Just shove in the tablets and see where it all goes from there. Fingers crossed they'll settle soon. For their sake,' no longer rings true. Even that we thought this way is a major reality check for us today.

Beryl's story ...

Just to give you an example of staff not celebrating the daily wins or valuing staff contribution, I share with you the following story:

I went to a residential care home a few years ago to visit Beryl. Major organisational renovations had left her highly agitated and frightened throughout the day. For her, this had been an extremely traumatic experience. She was a difficult lady to engage with because she was in a constant state of fight or flight. On one particular day, I turned up and it was unusually quiet. I found Beryl and engaged with her. She even started to tell me a story. Now, I couldn't understand one word she was saying but her face was relaxed, and she appeared to be the calmest I had seen her. I enjoyed every moment of our connection and felt happy that she felt safe enough to sit with me and chat.

As I left, I spoke with the two key staff who were rostered in that area on that day. I said to them both, 'Wow!! Beryl is looking good today. This is the best I've ever seen her. That's fantastic!'

One of the staff members replied with, 'Yes, well, you would come on a good day.' I was taken aback wondering why we wouldn't celebrate a 'good day'. I then asked both staff whether they thought she was having a good day because they were both there. They looked at me blankly and said nothing.

Then one of the women said, 'No, because I was on yesterday and it was just chaos in here.' I said to her, 'I'm not talking about yesterday. I'm talking about today. Do you think Beryl is as calm as she is today because you're both here?' They again just looked at me blankly as though they didn't understand what I was talking about.

I was astonished. I was offering a compliment that was free for the taking and they couldn't see it. I refused to let it go and asked again, then finally the other woman answered with, 'I guess, maybe,' accompanied by a shrug of her shoulders. I felt saddened because these two staff members were quietly spoken. They didn't realise and couldn't grasp that the flow on effect from their demeanours had resulted in a tangible calmness throughout the care home that day. A ripple effect I could see reflected in Beryl.

Question for reflection …

Where did you first learn about dementia and what it was? Was it a firsthand experience supporting someone or through stories you'd heard from others? Think about when and how you officially learnt about dementia and its complexities.

The gift …

When things are happy and calm, that's when we also need to take a step back to see what's going on, who is around and what other factors are influencing this. Try to work out why. Is it noisy or extremely quiet? Who was rostered on? What were they doing or not doing? How were they doing it? How do we capture that and how do we bottle it? How can we bring it out when we need it most? How can I influence my environment; how can we together influence our environment? I hope that makes sense. If you live with someone, you know that if that someone is having a bad day it impacts on the whole house and everyone in it. Everyone feels it. And that's what's happening here every day.

'Management say we have to just get everything done. We don't have time for the nice stuff.'

* Care staff *

3 • Who is Dementia and what is it's story?

'... dementia may be seen as having the features of a disability, in the same way as other degenerative conditions such as Huntington's disease, multiple sclerosis or Parkinson's disease.'

- T. Shakespeare, H. Zeilig & P. Mittler, p. 1077

Let's personify Dementia for a moment. It's easy – we do it all the time. The world of Dementia (with a capital D) is a game where Dementia currently holds all the cards. It's not only in the dominant position, but it has a long and successful history of taking and being in charge. Let's just think for a moment what it would be like if we gave Dementia a voice. A voice that we could hear, connect with, and know who we are dealing with.

This is a disease that has said for a long time, 'I'm here and I hold all the power. I'll take away all hope and I'll create a wave of sadness and despair that will last for many years. I'll sever relationships and rock family dynamics, but I won't do it through the quickness of death, I'll do it painstakingly through the slowness of time. I'll slow the clock down so that every day brings with it struggle, despair, heartache, and a sense of defeat. I, Dementia, will be the ultimate victor. I'll take away all hope by manifesting myself in many different incurable forms, so many that you won't know where to start in finding a cure for the destruction I'll cause.'

It's a disease that gloats, 'Where other diseases bring with them a sense of hope, a hope that the person they impact may be one of the lucky ones to survive, I don't bring those same odds. I come with a roulette wheel where everyone loses. No one wins except for me. The wave of destruction I cause and leave behind me will never be forgotten; the scars I leave will run deep. I'll make sure my legacy lives on and that none of you will ever forget me.'

What if we sat down with Dementia and asked it if there wasn't something we could do, to alter the path, to provide at least a glimmer of hope to all involved in its deadly tirade? Why couldn't there be a path for which the outcome is not known, one that we may influence on a day-to-day basis rather than spend the days waiting for the inevitable. If we could have that conversation, what would Dementia tell us about its own past? If we analysed Dementia as we would a person, what would we see? I think we would see a very bitter and twisted individual, one that life has given up on, one that has not experienced love or acceptance and so decides that if it can't find happiness then no one should. It almost starts to sound 'Grinchish' in nature.

So maybe rather than fight Dementia, we need to empathise with it. If we knew this to be the background of a person, how would we approach them? I guess it really depends on whether we as individuals were prepared to hear their story, to take time to understand their perspective and to try to connect with them regardless of all the damage they were doing or had done. So, rather than fight and battle against Dementia, maybe we could see what it might look like to support Dementia, to try to understand Dementia. Now when I say understand Dementia I don't mean from a physiological perspective because that, fortunately, is already being done and continuing to be understood. What I mean is, to understand why and how it takes over the life of a person and why it would wish that individual so much destruction. If we were to change our way of thinking, ever so slightly, then suddenly we find ourselves facing a new battle.

It's time to park the battle we've been having for so long, to fix and cure Dementia (leave that to the scientists) and to think differently, to work with, rather than against it. At the end of the day if we continue to try to fix, manage and control Dementia, what we ultimately end up doing is assisting it in its quest. We end up feeling bitter and resentful that we aren't really making any real difference. We end up causing further destruction to innocent individuals and their families. They're the innocent victims in all of this and that's why our thinking needs to change.

The image of dementia for so many is of an older individual with a vacant look on their face with family sadly by their side. That's not dementia. It remains tucked up and well hidden within the confines of a person's brain. It's so well concealed that we cannot see it for what it truly is, a destructive and horrible disease that has as its sole purpose, the need to destroy brain cells. That's it in a nutshell. It's a disease. Dementia cannot itself think about impacting on someone's personhood and well-being. It doesn't set about destroying families and relationships with others. Dementia doesn't stop the person living, it can't take away who the person is at the very core. So why then do we as a society give up on the person so soon?

We give dementia too much power, we give it too much control and we give it too much recognition for what it can do to people. Don't get me wrong, it's a horrible destructive disease that ruins lives but that's only part of the story. Think about it again. If dementia had a goal, what would that be? It would be to destroy brain cells. That's it, and it deserves no further acknowledgement or recognition beyond that, because if we do, we take away hope, we take away any possibility that things could or should look differently moving into the future. We throw in the towel before we have even begun to try.

The truth about dementia

The time has come to finally see that the way this insidious disease affects a person and the way it impacts on the life of an individual isn't the same for everyone experiencing it. It's not predictable like, for example, the flu, where we know that the person who is infected by another person will go through pretty much the same incubation period. They will experience the same set of symptoms and hopefully, all things going well, will come out the other end within a particular time period. Dementia doesn't follow a similar pattern. How it impacts someone can't be mapped and followed for care to be tailored in a more succinct way. This is a disease that follows no rules or patterns or trajectory. It's not a one size fits all syndrome, yet that's how we treat it. This life limiting disease with over 100 different possible causes is commonly referred to collectively as dementia.

This is where I step in, and I do so because I, along with many others, have worked with, supported, and treated people living with dementia who were all individuals who never looked how we first thought someone with dementia would look. And the reason for this was because they looked 'normal'. They didn't fit the image I and society had been conditioned to think was the face of someone living with dementia. My preconception of what dementia would look like meant there have been many people who have walked through my life who I never even knew had it. And the reason for appearing normal was quite simple, it was because regardless of their diagnosis, they were and continued to be 'normal'. I couldn't see the disease hiding covertly in their brain tissue. Dementia is good like that; it creates a stigma so great and has a power so mighty that we believe we have seen it. The only people to have ever truly seen this disease are those working in scientific laboratories looking through the lens of a microscope.

So why do we give dementia so much power? Because we've been preconditioned with the notion that there's nothing that we can do about it. We believe dementia just does its own thing, and we must learn to juggle the outcomes the best way we can. As I highlighted in the previous chapter, Dementia may turn off the lights but when you spend long enough with someone you very much see that someone is still home. On the surface the person may appear gone, but inside, at the core, there is certainly someone still there.

Dementia destroys brain cells, full stop. I know I keep harping on about it, but we need to use that as our starting point because the rest is up to us. The damage that this disease causes is not uniform. If you studied two different brains affected by the same type of dementia, they would be damaged in different ways, a different progression that's likely affecting different areas of the brain. So, because of that fact alone, how can we possibly treat and support people in the same way if the effects they're experiencing are totally different?

It's like saying that all cancers are the same and because of that we could save a lot of money and resources by treating, supporting, and managing the condition in the same way as the next person. For starters, we would never be that disrespectful. The person living with cancer firstly deserves to know exactly what type of cancer they have, and they would be offered an individualised treatment and management plan tailored to the exact presentation they were facing. They would even be offered individualised support for the type of cancer they had. This is how any individual with any medical condition should be treated.

Someone living with dementia still to this day, is not necessarily put through a full assessment process, one that comes with a conclusive diagnosis. There are still many instances where someone, somewhere, had a guess that the older person's confusion was 'likely' dementia. Why? Because they were over 65 years of age, and it was likely the most probable cause. Wrong!! So many individuals miss out on being treated for treatable conditions that were missed because someone thought it 'likely' they had dementia.

Now, if the person does actually have dementia, do they know what's causing it? Sometimes, and sometimes not. It's still not uncommon to see on a patient's or resident's case notes that they have 'dementia' or 'short term memory loss' or 'cognitive impairment' or 'cognitive dysfunction' or similar. That spot in the notes is for a clinical diagnosis and it was never designed for just having a guess. But if it is for someone with a type of dementia, then that seems to be more acceptable.

So, how can staff provide tailored care for someone living with dementia and individualise their treatment when they are not provided with all the information they need? They just can't. Everyone living with dementia, whether they are properly diagnosed or not, are all treated exactly the same: a cookie cutter approach that sees everyone receiving exactly the same treatment and care as the next person, regardless of the complexities and unique presentation of their individual cause. The responsibility for a conclusive diagnosis is not the responsibility of care staff who do their absolute best and achieve some amazing things, but do so blindly. They do so much with so little education in the different types of dementia and how to provide individualised care. They are likely to not even know what type of dementia the person they are supporting has. Just to add further disappointment, family members don't always know either.

Margaret's story ...

I remember during my years as a hospital RN. I had come in for an early shift, and handover commenced. I was told that I would be caring for a lady named Margaret who had come in during the night unwell and had advanced dementia. I was told that the emergency department had been so busy that her history was sketchy and there were no further details to add.

I met with Margaret and her speech was mumbled but she appeared alert. I spoke with her and told her I would be looking after her and I noted a vacant expression on her face. I took this as an indicator of her advanced dementia and had determined there was no way I was getting her up out of bed on her own. During the morning, I cared for Margaret and assisted her with personal care and her meals. It was mid-morning when I took a call from her son enquiring how his mother was. I told him she was resting comfortably and that she had eaten well. I advised him she had not been seen on the ward yet by the doctor. He then asked if he could speak to her. I thought how sweet it was that he wanted to speak to his mum knowing she would not have the ability to speak back coherently.

That's when things took an interesting turn. I explained to him that the ward phone was connected by a cord and I was unable to get it to his mum. He asked if she couldn't just get up and walk to the phone. That's when alarm bells starting ringing for me. The lady I was nursing could not have easily walked to the phone. I asked her son more about Margaret's daily life to which he described a woman who was fully independent, lived on her own, her cognitive function fine and no issues with her mobility. As luck would have it the doctor arrived so I told her son I'd need to call him back. I explained to the doctor what had happened. Urgent blood tests were ordered, and it was discovered that Margaret's sodium levels were not as they should be. This had resulted in her extreme confusion and presentation.

I share this story because it's so easy to jump to the conclusion that someone has dementia rather than exploring what else might be going on for them. I took the word of someone else that Margaret had advanced dementia and that was not the case. It is important to also note that people living with dementia get sick too. They are at risk of things going untreated because it is thought that whatever symptoms they have must be part of their dementia.

Question for reflection ...

Is dementia truly deserving of the power we ultimately give it?

The gift ...

We now know dementia makes life more challenging for a person, but it doesn't take away who they are. This was confirmed for me many years ago when a man living with dementia stood up at a community forum and said, 'You know, it's really weird because I know I've got dementia, but I still feel like I'm normal ...'

'We just don't have enough time or resources to make a real difference.'

• Care staff •

4 • Getting to know the real person

'Making a life history book is a very enjoyable and rewarding process, leading to a 'valuable resource which will help you to interact with the person with dementia as well as remembering what makes them unique.'

- M. Keynes & N. Kucirkova, p. 877

Who is the person living with dementia? This is a much more complicated question than it appears. Because we still know so little about the disease, we create this big monster that we need to manage and control. We end up trying to manage and control the person within whom the disease has chosen to reside. When we fail to incorporate an ongoing review into daily practices, we give up on the person and the disease wins. People suffer needlessly because dementia has silenced them, but more significantly, we have silenced them. We've taken away the voice they once had, the voice they have used throughout life to let the world know what their needs and wants were, what their fears and dreams are, what makes them feel happy, comfortable and content.

Think for just a moment how that might feel. Think again about that dream you've had where you're trying to talk but no one can hear you or the words don't come out as intended. It's even worse if that dream is a nightmare. Think of that dream, and the relief you feel when you wake up. Think of living with dementia where that dream is your actual daily reality – day after day.

The person living with dementia is an everyday person just like you and me. What happened for them was a change in circumstance that saw them start to experience challenges to their cognition. It's an experience that could happen to any of us. The challenges may have included changes to their short-term memory. They may be slower with their thought processes and what you see is an everyday, normal person who now struggles a bit more to integrate into daily life. I'll be honest in saying that I come from a place that I know very little about, and that is, what it's like to have dementia. I say that, because at no stage, do I want to come across or leave the impression that I know what it's like to have dementia. But what I have witnessed first-hand is dementia impacting on a person's self-esteem and confidence right from the time of diagnosis.

We think of the person with dementia as being equipped to carry the responsibility of being able to integrate their disease and cope with daily life. If they can't manage, then we assume they need to go into a 'facility' because they require high care. The onus is on us to be able to support people better to live an independent life. We can create a support mechanism so it is not just about the person with dementia but also about us learning how we can better help support rather than standing back wondering what to say or do.

There's a fear factor for all of us that we'll get it all wrong. But what the person with dementia craves most is normality, a world that resembles, in some way, shape or form, the world they were physically and emotionally forced to leave behind. They want a world where support systems help them to stay independent, ones without pity and unnecessary over the top special treatment. Quite often what is needed is more tailored support that doesn't single out the person but steps in like you would for a friend providing hope that they can be treated and interact like anyone else.

Moments can be overwhelming for people with dementia; so how can we better support them and make their life that bit easier? What might life be like for someone with dementia being out in a public space? Picture yourself on your own in a foreign country where people don't speak the same language as you. How would those around you know or understand what you need or want culturally, or what you need to feel safe and comfortable? How would you connect with those people and how would they go about connecting with you? Would you just give up and say it's just all too hard? Dementia, for many, is like finding yourself in a foreign country surrounded by people speaking a language that you don't know or no longer understand. There may be some key words you pick up, but because they speak so fast you just feel lost.

Dementia perspective

What does life with dementia look like from the person's perspective? This is a difficult disease to understand because often the person is unable or unwilling for fear of stigmatism to share their experiences. When this happens, we find ourselves doing a lot of guess work. For those of us who have worked in other areas of health or aged care and with people who don't have dementia, patients can tell us what it is they're experiencing. For example, someone who has cancer can tell us how terrible it is, how sick or nauseated they feel or how much pain they are in. They can talk about their impending surgery and how uncertain the future is. They can express how the cancer impacts on their family and ability to work. They can even get quite vocal and express how angry they may feel about it all.

We hear their spoken words or see their physical responses. We know what they're going through stinks and we may make some sort of connection with them. We think back and relate their experiences to times in our own life when we have been sick or unwell or in excruciating pain. We think about how horrible that must be. We make an empathetic connection with that person and because we understand their experience on some level, we are more likely to make allowances for that person's outburst. We understand why they express themselves angrily. They have every right to be angry at the situation they find themself in.

Our connection with dementia seems different. Where in our own lives have most of us experienced something even remotely like dementia? Many of us have gone through life without having had any type of amnesic event, times where we are not sure where we are or who the people around us are. These are frequently the experiences of the people we are supporting; so if we don't understand their world, how on earth can we connect with it? By reflecting on what it might it be like to have dementia and to walk in the shoes of another, we stand a greater chance of finding the answers we so desperately seek.

Listening to that which cannot be heard

How hard must it be living in a world where you know things should make more sense but over which you have no control; to be constantly disconnected from your environment and those around you? How does one truly live with the unrelenting confusion? We are learning something new every day in this area and listening to the person is a helpful start. For too long it has been us who have done the thinking, the talking and the feeling for them. Professional training for any support provider has historically focused on how we manage, control, and care for the person with dementia.

Now there is an opportunity to flip things around and to ask ourselves what does the person with dementia see when they see the care we are trying to provide? How do they see and interpret the environment around them? Do they like what they see, and does it make them feel safe and comfortable? Let's try and look at things from their perspective. When I use the term 'care' it's not just about the clinical components but also those providing a service from care-workers, maintenance, cleaners, laundry, and catering. It is not uncommon for some of these staff to have some of the more special connections.

Often those of us in more clinical or caring roles will attempt to connect with the disease instead of the person. And because of this we often lose. How rewarding would it feel providing people living with dementia with roles and purpose but not just by spending the day folding serviettes? I've heard of residents being paid in fake money for the jobs they have done and how angry and devalued the person feels thinking they're being ripped off for all their hard work. We are talking about a disease that affects memory and thought processes, not a person's feelings of self-worth.

Life in a bubble

Imagine how it would feel to live with relentless frustration and/or fear. When we take a moment to reflect, it doesn't take long to gain insight into why this might suddenly appear to us as anger or aggression and why things are likely to escalate.

People can feel disconnected from their environment and those around them, unable to contribute or be a true part of the fabric. In this task focused world, the person living with dementia is responding to a place not too dissimilar to a boot camp!

Blinds are up at 7am, voices in the corridor increasing in volume. There is a rushed shuffle. The person needs to be up, have had their breakfast, showered and ready for 9am. Ready, that is, to wait for lunch time to come around. The flow on effect is certainly a well-oiled machine, but at what cost? Is this how we define a life lived well? Is this the picture of a productive retirement? How many people living with advancing dementia would have chosen this life for their later years? I am guessing none. It's certainly not on my bucket list and I'm guessing not yours either. So our goal is to not overwhelm someone with a cognitive deficit but provide support instead. A person with dementia does not start their day by planning out what they are going to do but spends each waking moment just trying to navigate the moment that they're in. They will struggle with all the instructions and expectations thrust at them on any given day.

Personal impact

Having been fortunate enough to have worked with people newly diagnosed with dementia, I have been privileged to share in so many insights into the world they now face - the mourning for the loss of the person they thought they were and for the place they held within their family unit; and the change in dynamics within the relationships they have with others. Up to the time of diagnosis, the person is just like any other member of their local community. They may have been working in a long-term job, running a household, and looking after the family budget. They may also be with a partner with whom they shared the load of life.

A diagnosis of dementia dramatically changes a person's life as they know it overnight. The partnership they are in changes; the person that has walked through life by their side and referred to as their partner is now labelled their 'carer'. The person themselves is now referred to as 'the patient'. Even if they aren't in hospital or at their local GP clinic, this becomes their new label. This often begins from day one and it's a label that is never an easy one to shake.

People living with dementia have shared with me that those around them talk differently. They hear the comments made within earshot, others thinking they don't realise what's happening to them, that they aren't aware of the changes they now experience. The person with dementia does know something is not right and they try to protect their vulnerability for as long as they possibly can, something we all do. Those impacted by dementia still have aspects of their memory that are functioning. There are different ways that we remember things and dementia doesn't fully take away certain abilities overnight.

I've had clients share with me that they often withdraw from social opportunities for fear of looking stupid. They're aware that there are those around them who have said and will continue to say, 'I've already told you that five times' or 'you've already said that ten times.' Those comments are tucked away early on and for many it becomes easier to just stop talking or trying to connect with others than to risk the humiliation. This can happen well before the disease takes their ability to do so.

It's interesting, isn't it, when you think about someone you've supported over a long period of time and they've never said a word. We automatically think about the reason being dementia. The contradiction then comes when one on one time is spent with someone and you are talking to them using a meaningful tone or dialogue. It is not uncommon for the person to suddenly speak or attempt to speak. The words may be a bit jumbled or the words may not be in the right context, but the win is that the person is attempting to connect with you. When provided with the right set of circumstances and opportunity, connection can be made.

While trying to connect with what it might be like to live with dementia, consider the following. Be honest with yourself. You may want to say your responses out loud to yourself or share the questions in a conversation with others.

Imagine if …

You are sitting in a comfortable chair. From out of nowhere, someone starts speaking to you in a fast and jumbled voice. They are standing really close to you and their face not far from yours. You miss what they say even though they are speaking quite loudly. The expression on their face could be construed as anger. You think for a moment and know that you haven't done anything wrong and you're confused as to why they would be angry at you.

The voice gets louder and louder and the person is pointing at you and then pointing into the distance at something. You have no idea what they're saying or what they want from you, but you are beginning to feel uncomfortable. You start to feel more and more uptight because you just want to go home, and you want the noise to stop. You try to speak but the words won't come out as they should.

The person grabs your arm and starts to pull you. You now feel scared and upset. You don't even know who this person is.

How would you likely respond in this situation?

As you are pulled to a standing position by the stranger, you feel unsteady and feel like you might fall. You instinctively reach out to grab onto something, anything. The only thing you can connect with is someone's arm. You hold on tightly for some sort of security. Still feeling unsteady, two more people appear in your face and they're shouting something at you. You hope it's a dream, but something tells you it's all real and is not going to end there.

How do you think you would be feeling?

How would you likely respond?

When looking from the perspective of another, their responses and their connection to the world around them suddenly starts to make a bit more sense. Whether we're aware of it or not, we are walking past people living with dementia every day at the shopping centre, the supermarket, the library, your local park, or school. People are living with dementia and they might not even be aware of it yet themselves. Clients have told me that they were able to look back on the last ten or so years and during that time they knew something wasn't quite right. They just assumed or were told that it was just a sign that they were getting older. To compensate, they just wrote a few more lists or used their calendar a bit more regularly. What they never wanted to believe was that it could have been the earlier stages of dementia.

Who is the person living with dementia?

She is a mother, sister, daughter, niece, granddaughter. He is a father, brother, nephew, grandson. He is a husband, never married, a widower. She is a wife, a partner, a friend. She worked hard within the home, outside of the home, within her local community. She has lived through wars, pandemics, recessions, hard times, good times, sad times, challenging times. He has been to war, struggled to make ends meet, been a prominent member of his local community. He went to university, he finished high school, he left school early to provide for his family. She went to school, she went to college, she went to university. They deserve points for just showing up.

They don't need to prove themselves, they don't need to be anyone different, they don't need to conform. They just need the peace of mind knowing that it's their turn to be cared for, nurtured and supported and to feel safe. They are still people with wishes and hopes, regrets, and fears. They continue to grieve for those they have lost along the way and for the lives they once knew. They look at you knowing you have no idea who they are because they can see it in your face, and they can hear it in the tone of your voice. They hear you say you've had a long day, that you're over it and that you want to go home.

But she has become the person with dementia in room 3 and he is room 8.

Betty's story ...

Many years ago, I worked within a care home and did a regular Wednesday evening shift. I was responsible for the residents that only required a single staff member. Every Wednesday was pretty much the same for me and I generally followed the same routine. Each week I would work with a gorgeous lady named Betty. Betty was one of the most beautiful women you could imagine. She had a soft gentle face, and she would stroke my cheek and say lovely words of endearment. Everyone adored Betty and she was a pleasure to work with. Each Wednesday as I started my shift it would always begin with handover. Every week I would hear how Betty had been a bit agitated throughout the afternoon and to just keep an eye on her. I, along with other staff, instinctively knew that there was nothing wrong with Betty. She was just getting tired and didn't like to be rushed as the day wore on. I would always leave Betty until the very last to settle.

I knew her well enough to know that she didn't want to go to bed too early and that she just liked to sit and watch the business of the evening as things settled for the night. Every Wednesday night I would take her back to her room and sit her on the edge of her bed. I would tell her I was going to get her changed ready for bed and she would smile and say, 'Yes'. Every Wednesday night I would reach out to undo her top and every Wednesday night she would then become quite rigid. I would feel her tense up and I sensed that she was likely to hit me or try and push me away. I didn't want to get hit, so I would step back and stop talking.

My weekly ritual would then commence. I would walk over to her wardrobe and open it. I would pull out two dressing gowns still hanging in the wardrobe and hold them out for her to see. Every Wednesday I would say to her, 'What's it going to be Betty, the pink or the blue one?'

And every Wednesday night without fail she would smile and reply, 'Pink is my favourite colour,' and I would reply, 'Pink it is then.' I would walk back around to her where her smile would be from ear to ear. She would talk about what a beautiful colour pink was. I would then ask her about her relationship with her mum whom she had been extremely close to. She loved to talk about how much she loved her mum and how much she loved helping her mum. With no resistance I was able to change her, settle her and tuck her into bed. We never strayed from the script and I knew the words and things that would bring her comfort.

My biggest fear was that one day I would open that wardrobe and the pink dressing gown would not be there. It was such a key element to connecting with her and gaining her trust.

So, how many colleagues did I share this gem of a routine with? Not a single person. I was new in my career and this routine certainly didn't add any clinical value to her care. I also didn't want others to think I was professing to be some sort of dementia whisperer or something.

This is where confusion quite often lies as Betty would smile and say yes to getting changed, but her body language would always contradict this. Her body language would very clearly say no. Had I persevered, I undoubtedly would have been hit as I knew had happened to others on previous occasions. It was likely that Betty hadn't understood what I had initially said but still nodded politely as she was accustomed to doing. My job was to give her the space she needed and try to help her connect.

Question for reflection ...

Think about all the things that have happened in your life to bring you to this point in time: your family, culture, beliefs, and experiences. How would you then feel having lived a full and productive life to one day only be known as 'the person who often got angry?'

The gift ...

Understanding and connecting with the perspective of someone living with dementia decreases the likelihood of them being put in a position where they feel scared or alone.

'He thinks he needs to go and bring the cows in and I keep telling him the cows are all gone now and that he doesn't live on the farm anymore ...'

• Care staff •

5 • Context

'A more inclusive social model approach would ask: do mainstream services (health, transport, housing) place barriers in the way of people with dementia? Do people receive equal treatment? Is there 'reasonable adjustment' to the needs of people with dementia?'

- T. Shakespeare, H. Zeilig & P. Mittler, p. 1081

If we move the focus off dementia, we can review the concept of context more readily. Context is something that we can take for granted. Without it, we would never set foot outside our front door. This is because the world out there can be an unsafe place to be. There are good people out there but there are also people who will choose to cause us harm. How do we differentiate between the two? Without context, the world becomes a confusing place for us all.

We assume that because we have context that everyone has it. Just because Mrs White has lived in the same care home for the last three years, doesn't mean she knows where she is or who you are. Consider how you might respond to someone who walks up to you, introduces themselves and then tells you they're going to pull your pants down. It would be quite weird and creepy. This will likely be Mrs White's experience too.

Understanding context must be our starting point for changing and adjusting our thinking about the person living with dementia. Knowing context and how it impacts our own everyday existence creates a solid base for moving forward. The challenge with making a connection with someone living with dementia is that many of us don't have any benchmark for what it might be like. The concept is totally foreign. Most of us have gone through our whole lives never having had an amnesic type of event that leaves us not knowing where we are or who the people around us are. We go through our everyday lives being orientated to some degree or another. It's different from having had big Friday or Saturday nights where a few hours may be difficult to remember.

Therein lies the big and tangible difference between our everyday experience and that of someone living with dementia. Context is everything. Context is what keeps us feeling safe and connected. Let me give you an example. When I go to a care home for the first time, I generally see a sign out the front that tells me I'm in the right place. Because I have context, I walk straight through the front doors feeling quite safe. This is because context helps me throughout my day. I will subconsciously continue to do risk assessments, so I don't place myself in harm. I know through context that a care home is a relatively safe environment. I know that it's going to be full of older adults, along with people who provide care. I don't hesitate to go through those doors. Even so, my fully functioning brain needs to constantly remind me where I am. Often environmental cues start to change and after walking through those doors it's much easier for me to become disorientated. This is because the sign as to where I am is still out there on the footpath. It takes time for my brain to adjust to new surroundings.

I remember going into a care home where as soon as I entered, there was a reception desk, a café, and a hairdressing salon. Without context and memory, I might consider that I'm now in a shopping centre or hotel. Context will remind me that I'm still in a care home. There are times when I'm training care staff and it's not uncommon to find myself in a room adorned with a lot of religious memorabilia, crosses, pictures of religious figures and vases of fake flowers. I will challenge staff to take a moment to reflect on what that room may look like to them if context was taken away from them. It only takes a moment for the connection to be made that we are no longer in a care home but now in a chapel, a church, or another place of worship.

With the door to that room closed, context will inform me that the care home still exists on the other side of the door. Without context, how do I know if harm awaits me, or that it could lead straight outside. We can thank our healthy brains for constantly keeping us orientated and updated as to what's going on around us.

Now think about those around us with a dementia diagnosis. When I'm training a group of 20-30 staff, who I've never met before, I may feel a little nervous, but I always feel safe in their presence. This is because, although I've never met them, context tells me they are all likely to be staff from a particular organisation and they are there to hear me speak. Take away context and I then find myself being stared at directly by 20-30 people. What a daunting prospect, one that would instantly raise alarm bells for me! For those with advancing dementia, it's not a normal phenomenon and likely to make them feel instantly uncomfortable or even unsafe with a group staring at them.

Context helps to make sense of this situation. Why would 20 people just stare at me? Without context I am likely to feel self-conscious and may even start to feel trapped or confined. This comes down to our fight or flight response and I'm now on high alert for how I can get out of there. If I found that the door was locked, my anxiety levels would likely skyrocket. How might one respond if told to get away from the door? What if during my heightened state of fear, someone tries to get me to come and play bingo? What might my response to you be?

What's interesting to note is that it only takes one person staring at me to grab my attention, to make me start to feel self-conscious. I try to work out why. I think to myself, 'Is there something hanging out of my nose? Did I slop my lunch down the front of me?' But then I notice that two people are staring at me. We are all wired to take note of moments like these and to see them as a potential red flag. If the two people start whispering to each other, I will definitely think it's about me. I start wondering what they're talking about or what they might be planning.

The thing that confirms my suspicions, is when one or both people look directly at me and in a long and drawn-out high-pitched voice with an upward infliction and exaggerated smile say something like, 'Hellooo, how are you today?' My suspicions are instantly confirmed. I now know that something is definitely going on and it likely involves me. Have you found yourself walking through the shopping mall when someone steps in front of you and says, with a not dissimilar high-pitched and drawn-out voice, 'Hellooo, how are you today?' What do you instantly think? Are your suspicions instantly roused? Are you thinking along the lines of, 'What does she want from me?' or 'What's she trying to sell?'

Another example may be a little closer to home: Think of your current living situation. You live with family, a partner or maybe a housemate. You've been at work all day and you are entering through your front door. A person that you live with greets you at the door and says something along the lines of this, 'Hi, how was your day? You must be exhausted, let me take your bag so you can get comfortable. Can I get you a drink or something to eat?' What are your immediate thoughts?

Do you think, 'Oh what a lovely and thoughtful family I have?' Or are you more likely to think something along the lines of, 'What do you want? What have you done? Or how much do you want?' Whenever anyone is extra nice to us, we are instantly suspicious of their possible intentions. Unless you know them or have context for what's going on, you instantly distrust the person's motives. You may even go into defensive mode.

Isn't it interesting that we often find ourselves going around a care home, all day saying, 'Hellooo Beryl, how are you today?' while expecting Beryl to have context. Think about Beryl's facial expression when you say that to her. Think about how she responds when you add something like, 'I've been looking for you everywhere.' It's a comment that puts us all naturally on the back foot wondering why someone would be looking for us and using our name. We must keep in mind that something that is intended to be a friendly gesture has the potential to really unsettle someone. How might you respond to the person that does this to you in the shopping centre?

Who are you?

I'm hoping that you're starting to make the connection to a world without context. How much uncertainty is someone left with; to be left not knowing where you fit in but highly aware of the actions of others around you. There is also an assumption that because I've worked in that care home for the last two years that Beryl knows who I am and what I do there. It's an unrealistic expectation to put on someone that is living in many cases without context due to advancing dementia.

How does Beryl know who we are? Is it because of the uniform that may be worn? If you do wear a work uniform, I want you to look at yourself in the mirror. Who do you see? What is it about your uniform that will tell me who you are and what your job is? In most cases, the only way I'll know, is for you to tell me what you do and for me to then remember that information. Uniforms over the years within the nursing and care industries have been quite generic. There can be a shirt worn that looks identical to one seen in any other occupation. Is it fair to expect someone with a compromised memory to retain that information every moment of every day?

I'm not suggesting a change in uniform, but I am suggesting we don't take it for granted. Don't rely on it telling your story. Unless your uniform is distinctive then nobody knows what you do unless you tell them. You see a police officer in uniform standing in the middle of an intersection. Because of what he is wearing, you are unlikely to say something like, 'What's that idiot doing standing in the middle of the road?' His uniform instantly tells you what he does, and you will assume there's been some sort of traffic incident.

Now you may be thinking that these examples are not necessarily accurate; that when you work with Mrs Brown she knows exactly who you are. She even remembers when you've been away on days off. There are different ways that we remember and just because Mrs Brown remembers your face doesn't mean that she knows your name or what you do. This is the assumption that we make and it's often one that can get us into trouble. Just because someone remembers your face or your name, doesn't imply permission or consent to just launch into personal care. For any of us there must be trust and a connection established, along with the all-important, context. This needs to be the starting point before any of us would likely be receptive to any invasive or personal contact from others. The good part is that with conscious effort and consideration, it's something that is very achievable.

If we truly want to start moving forward, we need to have a better understanding of where the person is coming from. How can we better tap into their world?

Stepping into the unknown

So let's spin things around and look at things not just from our own perspective but more importantly from the other person's viewpoint. How does someone with dementia see us? How do they perceive their environment? How do they view the care we are trying to provide? Does any of this make sense to them? We make so many assumptions based on little understanding.

Imagine you're on holidays or staying at someone's house. You wake up at 2am and you spontaneously gasp. You do this because the light around the window isn't where it is in your bedroom at home. For just a few seconds, your heart rate is up because you're not sure where you are. The good thing is that your brain is constantly ticking over and although you're not sure where you are, you know that you are where you're meant to be and that you are safe. The best part is that you are able to reorientate yourself quite quickly and hopefully go back to sleep.

Now imagine if that gasping moment lasted not just for a few seconds but for a few hours. What if how you feel in that moment lasted for days or even months? How easy do you think it would be for you to connect with me during that time? It would be really difficult. How easy do you think it would be for you to connect with your environment? Yes, likely to also be quite difficult. That GASP moment has put you into a state of flight or flight (sympathetic response) and so this response becomes about survival. So, we can only be comfortable in any given situation if we can reorientate and know what's going on and make sure it's safe. If I cannot deem a situation as being safe, then I'm possibly at risk of harm.

This response is vital in order for us all to stay safe and even alive. That survival instinct is innate in all of us regardless of a disease process, so context becomes everything. It's easier for me to be able to relax into an environment and feel comfortable if I've got context. Imagine living without context not just for a few seconds or hours but living without it for months and years. This is what dementia can do to a person.

Life with context can be just as confusing

Once, I arrived at a care home to conduct staff training. I was told by the friendly receptionist that I just needed to head down to the boardroom. She assumed I had context and that I had been there before. When I clarified that I hadn't, she politely told me to just turn first right and head to the end of the corridor. From there, I needed to turn left, and it would be 'obvious' after that. I must emphasis that she was nothing short of helpful and I felt comfortable with her demeanor. But she assumed that I had context.

I headed off and turned at the first right but found myself standing in a doorway to a big open office. That wasn't right, so

I went to turn at the next 'first' right and there before me was a lift. She hadn't mentioned anything about a lift, so I assumed that wasn't right either. I continued to the next 'first' right, which led to the beginning of a long corridor. Was this finally my 'first' right? Well, confusion set in for me because on the door to the corridor it said, 'Therapy centre – do not enter – wait in waiting area for staff.' What was I to do? I tried the next 'first' right. I'm now up to the fourth one and that didn't look right either. What was interesting to note was that my pride stopped me from going back and asking for clarification. The receptionist had given me a simple instruction and I felt that I should be able to work it out. I felt the pressure to sort it out on my own. I looked around for a sign and saw nothing that would guide me to my intended destination.

It was then that I saw a staff member and asked her where the boardroom was. I felt defeated when she said that she didn't know either. It was now time to swallow my pride, go back to reception and humbly say I had failed the simple instruction. This may all sound a tad melodramatic but it's true. I was there as someone to impart knowledge to others and I couldn't even locate the room to do it in. I felt somewhat appeased when she smiled and told me it was the third right I needed and that even though the sign said 'Do not enter', that I could go on down. It made me realise that if I had so much trouble following the instructions, someone with dementia didn't stand a chance! These are the ambiguous instructions we often casually give to people and assume that they have the context to navigate them, forgetting that they may not.

Context in another context

There are so many different angles to the importance of context. Another moment where things could have ended with a very different outcome for the person was during my ambulance days. I was frequently tasked to the city where a large homeless population would gather. Over many months I had often been sent to assist Steve when bystanders would report a collapsed man in a public area. Because of this I had gotten to know Steve and knew that he had been living on the streets for a while. I had also learnt that he had a long-term brain injury and a history of diabetes.

Steve was an amazing individual in that he could still function with an almost non-existent blood sugar level. He did not function well, but he certainly didn't go into a diabetic coma like someone presenting in a similar way would. Instead, Steve would become incredibly angry and would come out swinging. When his blood sugar levels were back under control he returned to the most gentle and polite individual you could imagine. This was Steve's life on the street and unfortunately, this left him extremely vulnerable.

I was working a day shift when the call came through that a male had been seen running erratically through traffic and appearing quite aggressive. We were told police were also on their way. It was highlighted that substance abuse was the possible cause. Upon arrival, I identified straight away that it was Steve and that the police were already in attendance. They were attempting to get him off the road, but Steve would continue to run away. I knew that police had to act fast. They needed to manage the risk that Steve was causing to the public and motorists. I could see that the police were about to intervene in a way that would cause undeserved distress and possible harm to Steve.

I started to call out that Steve was likely having a medical event and that we needed to intervene immediately. The police struggled to comprehend this as their priority was, understandably, to get him detained as soon as possible. It just saddened me that Steve was about to be treated like a criminal. I had no desire to stop police, I just wanted them to have context. I continued to yell over the chaos that I knew Steve had a medical condition that he needed urgent attention for.

The police were wonderful and after apprehending him in the best way possible, they took him straight into the ambulance. A blood sugar reading showed he should have been in a diabetic coma. After treatment, Steve started to show signs of understanding what was going on. He was confused but as this subsided, the Steve we knew began to reemerge. He still had elements of confusion but was mortified to hear what he'd been doing.

It is so important to know the person and to know what makes them tick. This puts you in a good position to identify changes that may not be related to the person's dementia as soon as they become noticeable, to then act upon those changes immediately and become the voice for them in the moments where theirs may be lost. To know that you can tangibly influence the outcome for someone is a powerful tool that you hold. This wasn't about Steve's lack of context and it wasn't about mine. It was about the context within which those around Steve saw him and made judgement calls accordingly, judgements for him that would be the difference between him ending up in hospital or locked up in the nearby police cells and left without urgent medical treatment.

It wasn't the fault of police; they took what they saw at face value and acted on what needed to be done. But by adding context to the mix, they changed their tac and ensured that Steve was treated with respect. They had a clearer understanding that he required urgent medical attention. They knew that by working together as a team we were able to achieve that for him. This is why advocating for someone without a voice is so important because it impacts how others will see them and either attempt to connect or not bother. We don't want to see people just going through the motions of care provision.

Jeff's story ...

When the skill of providing context is mastered, it changes the whole game. The following happened when I was a paramedic working on instinct rather than a carefully thought-out plan.

On this day, we were called to a house where a man named Jeff was 'going off.' He had a diagnosis of dementia and the family had spoken to his GP who said he needed to go to hospital. As we arrived at the front of house, even before fully getting out of the ambulance, we heard a lot of shouting coming from inside. We noted that we were there for a man, but they were female voices that could be heard from outside. We approached with caution and were invited to come in. Once inside I saw a well-dressed man standing tall in the middle of the lounge room surrounded by three women all shouting at him. They were telling him very loudly that he had to go to hospital and each time someone said it, he would shake his head and say, 'I'm not going.' This made the women yell even louder at him and I started to feel more anxious than what Jeff appeared to be.

I found it amusing that the quietest person in the room was the person who had been said to be 'going off.' I called out for everyone to stop speaking as it was quite overwhelming. I asked for everyone except Jeff to leave the room so that we could talk. I stood in front of Jeff and his face looked calm as he quietly said to me, 'I don't understand what's going on.' I looked at him with as much sincerity as I could muster and replied, 'I'll be honest with you Jeff, I've got no idea either.' We exchanged a small smile of connection and I asked him if he would like me to tell him why I thought I was there. He nodded.

This is the point where things took a turn I wasn't expecting, because in the back of my mind I was not sure where we were all heading with this. How could I make someone go to hospital who clearly didn't want to go? I explained to Jeff that his doctor had asked for us to come and give him a lift to hospital as he wanted him to have a checkup. That was it. That was all I said. And with that, Jeff walked straight past me, past my partner and headed straight to the ambulance. He climbed in on his own and sat himself comfortably in a seat.

I was shocked that it had been so easy but, on reflection, I believe it was context that saved the day. The women in the room were telling him he was sick and needed to go to hospital. But standing before us was clearly a well man who did not appear or feel sick in the traditional sense. The words sick and unwell were not connecting with Jeff. He didn't feel sick, so he wasn't going to hospital. With our brief exchange, it appeared to make more sense. After all, well people do go for medical checkups.

Question for reflection ...

When someone appears confused with what you are saying, are you more likely to keep saying the same thing or adapt the instruction or conversation to meet the person where they're at?

The gift ...

By changing and influencing the dialogue around the person, we have the ability to reframe the thinking of others.

'I've told him numerous times that this is his home now.'

● Care staff ●

6 • Working with someone with dementia

*'Interpersonal skills that staff require, to work with, and for,
older people in a meaningful way, include sensitivity,
connecting emotionally and showing vulnerability.'*

- B. Dewar and T. MacBride, p. 1376

A lack of clear direction

As we've discussed earlier, dementia care is a difficult area
within which to support someone. It's not the person that's
difficult. It's their ability to communicate their needs and wants
that can be difficult. By looking from the person's perspective,
we not only empathise with their experience, but we end up
having more insight into how we can adapt our practice. We
have a better insight into how we can give back so much of what
appears lost. When life is seen through the eyes of the person, a
clearer understanding of their perspective presents itself. It
brings an insight into the impact of the disease and the losses
they've experienced.

Dementia is a physical disease of the brain and the person has actual damage that you can clearly see through a microscope. There are literally gaps and shrinkage where brain tissue should be. There are physical pieces missing. In the centre of the brain is the hippocampus. This is the area where our memories are housed and where Alzheimer's disease will start. If you think about memories being stored in a filing cabinet with the long-term memories being stored right at the back and the new memories in front, the experience of Alzheimer's disease is that most recent memories are the first memories lost. That's why someone may not recall that their son visited this morning but will often talk about the fishing trip they went on with their grandfather when they were a child.

It's always been important for me to visualise the damage that's been done to the brain by dementia. I do this through remembering a previously seen diagram (there are many available online). When I see a diagram of a brain with Alzheimer's disease, I refer to it as the plaster cast of the brain. For me, a plaster cast on someone's leg is a clear indication that something is broken. I instantly know that although the person has abilities, they currently also have limitations. I wouldn't expect that person to help me bring my shopping inside. I would adapt my expectations and my thinking to how I could better support them in accommodating their needs.

It's interesting to note that because we can't see the damage that dementia causes, there is often an expectation that the person should be able to remember: to remember routines, to remember how they are expected to behave and respond and to remember that there is a requirement to conform within the environment where they reside. Because we can't see the damage that the disease causes, we find it harder to shift our expectation and truly connect with individual limitations. As with context, there is an expectation that the person knows where they are and what they should be doing. All these expectations require a fully functioning brain with an intact memory and cognition in order to be met.

Pride and ego are something we all have, and it's not lost with dementia. None of us want the world to see our weaknesses or flaws and we cover them as best we can. Our whole world could be crumbling, but when someone asks us how we are feeling, we're likely to say something like, 'Fine. All good thanks.' We are likely to say this even when things couldn't be worse. We often cover up what we don't want the world to see and the person with dementia is also attempting to do the same. Someone with dementia will be trying to blend in and be just like everyone else. This creates confusion for us in understanding their limitations. It means we set the bar of expectation much higher than we would if we could see the physical effects of a broken limb or stroke. It's important to remember that the person is often struggling more on the inside than we ever get to see on the outside.

Institutionalised care

Have you ever pictured yourself living in institutionalised care? Imagine you're at home tonight watching your favourite show on the television. You're sitting in your favourite seat in your loungeroom. It's 8.20pm and I burst in telling you I am about to get you ready for bed. Annoying, isn't it! Because I'm a caring person, I will try not to interrupt your show, as I know there's still ten more minutes to go. I won't put you to bed straight away, I'll just help you get into your pyjamas until your show finishes. But then, you'll need to go to bed at 8.30pm because I've got a lot of other visits to do.

When posing this very scenario to groups I have worked with, a common reply is, 'I would tell you to get out!!' I act confused as to why you would speak to me like that. All I am trying to do is be friendly and to help. I was even smiling. Afterall, although you didn't invite me into your home, your well-meaning family asked me to come by and provide you with assistance. If you do tell me to get out and threaten me, do I document that as a resistive or aggressive behaviour? Why does it appear that the rules for me and the rules for someone with dementia are so different?

It is useful to remember that it's the person with dementia's home and they don't want me there intruding. It doesn't matter how much I respect that, without context they just want me gone. Perhaps they don't need me because they're able to change themselves? This may be true, BUT I believe I could do it quicker. I may find resistance or be yelled at. I may be confused by the person's response given my job is to care. I'm likely to leave thinking that the person was being quite difficult and unreasonable.

The picture portrayed here, despite a carer being friendly and well intentioned, is really about us inflicting well-meaning care on another human being and for them to just accept it. That's what we deem to be a successful transaction. The reality is that as well intentioned as we may be, not everyone wants the type of care we offer. Surely they would want a say in their care.

We need to consider how interesting it is that we work with people with dementia who in many cases let us know very clearly that they're not interested in the type of care that we want to provide. But when they refuse or protest, we quickly stamp it as a behaviour. How can it be that when you respond in a particular manner that's considered normal and even understandable, but it's not acceptable or normal for someone with dementia to express themselves in exactly the same way? Yes, this does get confusing.

Let's change the scenario a little. You're quite unwell or have sustained an injury that leaves you with mobility issues. Would you now be more receptive to the care I am offering you within your own home? Circumstances will always dictate how receptive we are to care. If it makes sense to us as being something we need, whether we like it or not, the path ahead is likely to be smoother. It all ties back to context again. Explain to the person you are supporting why you are doing something to them and not just what you are doing. Big difference.

Many people living with dementia whom you support do not identify as being sick or unwell. The person may know that something isn't right, but unless they're experiencing something like a headache or a stomachache, then they're unlikely to identify as being unwell and requiring care. It would be disconcerting for carers to appear daily and inflict care on them every single day. If someone had a toothache, it would be confusing to then have another person pulling their pants down. It would be difficult to see the relevance or connection.

I believe we need to start thinking differently about what it feels like to receive care; to think more about what it would take for us to allow another person, regardless of whether they were medical or not, to perform any invasive procedure on us. In the previous example, group members made it perfectly clear that without context they would flatly refuse my care. They would also have no hesitation in telling me so. Isn't this what someone with dementia might be trying to tell us by their behaviour? Therein lies the miscommunication. Just because the person may not be able to find the right words for what they want to express or even ad lib with something like 'f@&k off', we should take the time to listen to them as we would want others to do for us.

The apathetic model of care

Definition of apathy – (noun), Merriam-Webster Dictionary
Lack of feeling or emotion: lack of interest or concern.

Apathy is an area that is a big issue, particularly in the care home setting, but one that is rarely mentioned. Apathy can be seen in those that are withdrawn or who have, frankly, given up. Apathy will likely see widespread compliance and can be hailed for making any shift a good shift. Apathy can be seen in those sitting quietly and not causing any fuss, those with a vacant look and disconnection from life. This has been our long-standing benchmark for normalising what dementia looks like. This behaviour ensures that staff will be able to tick off all the things on their 'to do' list. But is that fair to the person with dementia? What does quality of life look like for them?

Think about the transitioning program you have in place for someone entering into care. Is there one? We all go through an orientation program when we start a new job. Imagine turning up day one of your new job and being told that you'll just have to settle yourself in. Someone shows you to your desk and you are expected to just work it out from there. It's interesting how quickly new residents are expected to comply with and adjust to the institutionalised care model without even being issued with a handbook. They are expected to fit in to a new routine with a new set of rules. Imagine being someone who has lived their whole life following 'the rules', only to then find themselves not even knowing what they are. Perhaps an orientation program for new residents with dementia would be useful.

When someone is compliant, they are seen as being 'fixed' rather than being even more broken than when they first came in. The spotlight then turns to the person who doesn't settle well, the one that becomes aggressive and wants to go home. There is an expected compliance from those living with dementia and workplace culture sees us needing to fix and manage the things that appear disruptive. Apathy on the other hand is commonly overlooked because it makes the job so much easier. When we look at apathy for what it really is, we see a lonely and lost individual who has given up on life, someone who no longer experiences any pleasures in their daily world. When we understand apathy and its impact, we find a whole new area opening up that needs to be addressed. We redefine what it is to experience a change to behaviour that should now include support for issues that were never previously seen. The wonderful part is that with conversation and planning we can all influence change in this space that sees people better engaged and connected than ever seen before.

How big should a warning sign be?

When you or I start to get agitated or angry about something our voice starts to change. If I stood up from my chair and yelled, 'I'm getting sick of all these interruptions,' everyone would hear me. When someone is getting upset or agitated near us what do you think it does to those around the person? It sees them more likely to back off, to heed the warning signs and give the person space. This might be physically moving away, or they just stop talking to the person. What's interesting to note is that if someone with dementia starts to get upset or agitated, what actually happens is that those around them are more likely to move in closer. This is a personal space that we know in normal circumstances is a no-go zone.

We know this is the case due to the number of injuries that occur to care providers. Personally, I'm going to move back because I have a fear of being hit. The thing is, that when someone starts to get agitated, they're entering into that fight or flight response. What that does is trigger something in us, it triggers our fight or flight response. Our brains put us on high alert and say, 'Whoa! Be careful. This situation might be getting out of hand. I might be in danger.'

When we are near someone who is becoming agitated, their voice is likely to start escalating in volume. Because we are experiencing the same response as they are, our voice is likely to start escalating in volume also. When both parties are becoming more and more agitated, those elevated stress levels often make it difficult to think of anything productive or useful to say. Often the best we can come out with in a stressful situation is to tell the other person to 'Calm down.' A classic default, 'You **need** to calm down.' It sounds like a request but it's actually code for, 'You're starting to make me feel uncomfortable and I need you to stop it.'

Now think about a moment in time when you've felt agitated or uptight and someone has said to you, 'Calm down.' How reassured have those words made you feel? Did you find those words calming or comforting? Did they assist you to actually calm down? Or was it more likely the case that your agitation escalated even further? Often the instructional commands of 'Calm down' or 'You need to stop' are accompanied by pointed finger waving. I know I would feel my stress levels going even higher.

It is difficult but not impossible to resist joining another individual in their escalating agitation. I think it was a survival skill I was quick to learn during my time as a paramedic. I couldn't allow myself to be drawn into the reactions of an individual as it would mean the difference between a calm and productive scene compared to one of chaos and disorder. I learnt from others that regardless of how I felt on the inside, the outside of me needed to reflect what the person needed from me most in that moment, to understand their distress and stand by their side during this time of crisis. Concentrating and training yourself to have a calm and reassuring presence increases the chances of a successful outcome with minimal distress.

This came into play for me at a time when I was presenting to a large community group. The room was predominately filled with family members supporting someone with dementia. Those with dementia were being accommodated in a different room. One man refused to leave his wife and was determined to stay in the group with her. I reassured her that it was OK. During the presentation the man had become restless and a worker tried to coerce him from the room. The man left the room with the worker but moments later the door flung open and he attempted to reenter. I knew things were going to go downhill quickly when the worker grabbed the man's arm and told him to come back out. The man wrenched his arm from the grip and stormed towards me shouting words that were incomprehensible. I had only a few moments to work out my response, but I trusted, stupidly or not, that he wasn't angry at me. I had no idea whether he was going to hit me or not, but I chose to stand my ground and say nothing.

As the man approached, I could hear the pain in his voice and although his volume didn't waver, I saw his facial expressions change. He stopped right in front of me and continued to talk in a raised voice with words I couldn't understand. But what I quickly realised (in front of a packed room) was that he thought I was in charge of proceedings, he thought I was the one he could voice his complaint to.

I let him continue and I didn't interrupt him. I ensured that while I felt rattled on the inside that all he would see on the outside was an expression of empathy and compassion, that he could see that I cared that he felt aggrieved and angry. I let him finish what he so desperately wanted me to hear. His voice eventually started to quieten and calm a little. It was then that I asked what I could do to help him. After discussing what had upset him in the first place, it turned out to be an item he thought he had misplaced. The end result was that he quietly returned to the seat next to his wife and continued as if nothing had happened. For me, the best thing was that no one interrupted or came to intervene. The man felt heard and that was all he had wanted. I don't necessarily recommend this approach as I will be honest and say I did feel threatened. What I did trust was my experience to read his body language and I truly believed that his anger wasn't directed at me.

Neil's story

It's so important to know and understand the person and what's important to them. How much do you really know about the people you support?

I remember working with a group and I was interested to know how much they knew about a specific resident called Neil. The group I was with really cared about their residents and had made me feel comfortable when I arrived. They were friendly and supportive of each other. But as well-intentioned as that is, it's not always enough. I told the group that I was going to ask them some questions about Neil to see how much they knew about him. My thoughts were to start with easy questions and work down to harder ones that may not have come up for them in everyday conversation.

I started with question one. What was Neil's wife's name? A silence swept over the room. Staff started looking around at each other. It was like they were willing the answer to miraculously appear from somewhere. But the answer never came. Nobody in that room knew the name of Neil's wife. I knew without a doubt that these staff cared about Neil, but they were missing some vital information that would enable them to better connect with him, information that would help Neil to know that those around him knew who he was at the core.

This seemingly basic information was a conversation starter for anyone who chose to use it. This information was readily available in his file, an accessible document that could assist staff to connect in ways they could never have imagined. This was a wonderful learning moment for staff. They could clearly see that what had been missing, the answers they had been seeking, had been staring them right in the face all along.

Question for reflection ...

If those around you only ever focused on your weaknesses and the things you couldn't do, think about how that is likely to leave you feeling?

The gift ...

By understanding the challenges that dementia specifically brings for a person places us in a better position to focus on the things that aren't broken.

'I just wanted to say that I am so moved that you have all sat here for this long listening to what it's like for us.'

* Care home resident *

7 • Communication & behaviours

'A knowledge-translation framework, information and strategies can be provided to family and professional caregivers to help them optimize residual memory and communication in people with dementia.'

- E. Smith, M. Broughton, R. Baker, N. Pachana, A. Angwin, M. Humphreys, L. Mitchell, G. Byrne, D. Copland, C. Gallois, D. Hegney and H. Chenery, p. 256

It would not be possible for me to fit all my learnings related to communication and changes to behaviours into one chapter. But it would be remiss of me not to highlight how these areas connect to our current discussion. The idea is to give back the aspects of a person's world that dementia has made so difficult for them to access: opportunities to reminisce about the past, to share hopes and dreams, to talk about things that may be concerning them, have all become so well-hidden, we often think that they're gone for good. We know this isn't always the case, so we need to look at how we can begin to get them back.

Communication and changes to behaviours are known to be heavily influenced and affected by dementia. And because of that, many things that fall under one or both of these categories often go straight into the too hard basket. Often, they'll stay there until someone prescribes a pill to try to fix them. These two areas are usually seen and discussed in isolation from each other. But the thing is, they are often more closely related and connected than we think.

It's not uncommon to hear people comment that someone living with dementia will lose the ability to communicate. Full stop. It's also common to hear it said that people with dementia have 'behaviours' which can be difficult to manage at times, without medication. Full stop. Let's explore these areas briefly.

Communication

Communication is so much more than just talking, listening, and saying something in return. It is the essence of connection and it's something that's not always easy to do. But things don't always go to plan. So, when we're supporting someone with dementia, we need to look at all options available to us to assist in clear communication.

We've discussed what the world of dementia might look like to the individual: so it goes without saying that it's us who need to adapt. To make someone feel comfortable, safe, and connected, the words that we use are only part of the story. If we want to create an inclusive environment for someone living with dementia, then all our interactions must be meaningful to them.

Meaningful conversations or dialogue are not just about walking into each person's bedroom and commenting on the weather. Comments along the lines of how lovely the weather is, or how cold or hot it is, or how much rain there is, are likely to leave others feeling disconnected. The person with dementia will be connecting in that moment maybe with the words you use but more so to your body language and tone of voice. These three areas need to match up or else the person is likely to shut off.

Think about it ...

We're often guilty of information overload in our daily lives. I run into a friend I haven't seen for a long time and the conversation may go something like this: 'Oh my gosh! How are you? How long has it been? What are you doing now? Are you married? Do you have any kids? We should catch up sometime. What days are you free?' My friend somehow captures all those questions and may reply with something like: 'Yes, it would have to be five years. I now work part time. I'm married now and have two kids. I don't work on Tuesdays so maybe we could catch up then.' In a blink of an eye, I've just launched six questions at her and she's replied accordingly.

Think about this in the care context. You walk into someone's room and say something like, 'Morning. How are you? Just getting you up for breakfast, and then we'll get you into the shower. Let me know which shirt you want to wear because your daughter is going to be here this morning. She's taking you out for a lunch with your granddaughter. How lovely is that? Time to get you up and sorted.' That's a lot of information for anyone to take in, let alone a person with dementia.

We're all guilty of dialogue overload. It's the way we live our everyday lives so we often don't think that it would be any different in this setting. It's likely that the person will smile and politely nod, and we take that to mean they've understood everything we've said. So, given that the person with dementia will struggle to process more than one instruction at a time, they likely didn't stand a chance. No wonder they're then likely to look confused when we try to push them into the shower.

The truth serum known as body language

Reading body language is one of the greatest tools at our disposal. The best part is that it works both ways. It's useful for people with dementia to read what we may be trying to communicate but it can also aid us to understand better what it is they are trying to express. I know this sounds pretty basic, but it's unfortunately so commonly missed.

It's not about the jumbled words that come from someone, but so often it is about the tone of voice and body language that go along with the words. When giving back the voice of someone with dementia, it is sometimes just the tone they are using and their body language that we need to understand and receive their message.

Those living with dementia have taught me not to get hung up on the words they may or may not be using to understand exactly what they're feeling or experiencing. I have learnt that the words are often misleading and not necessarily a reflection of the true story. But confusion, fear, happiness, sadness and anger are the messages we can read loud and clear if we just take time to listen.

We have the ability to become more perceptive - to have a better chance at reading situations as they are unfolding rather than waiting for things to end in a grand finale that no one understands; to better see things brewing and have the ability to do something about it before it escalates and takes over a whole situation. Maybe this was a skill I learnt more quickly when working in an emergency department or out on the road as a paramedic. When working with people with dementia it is an asset to be able to read situations quickly enough to be able to assess them, and to start implementing a possible solution even before the final facts are known. This is a skill that has the capacity not only to improve lives but to also save them.

I didn't see that coming

If agitation levels are increasing and remain unnoticed, then situations can escalate quite quickly. Two parties are suddenly in conflict and things can heat up. When stress levels continue to rise within a care setting, distinct outcomes can occur. Often what happens is that the person with dementia will be sedated and possibly restrained, while the carer goes on their tea break or stress leave.

This is a situation that becomes distressing for all involved but it's the person with dementia who becomes the person labelled as the problem. I remember hearing the sad story of a woman who would start to escalate with her agitation and, as staff started to surround her, she would yell, 'Go on! I guess you're going to jab me again.'

Could this situation have been dealt with any differently? For most cases, the answer is a resounding yes. There is a better way. We just need to learn to read the signs. What a difference this makes to the person with dementia. When we all start speaking with loud anxious voices ourselves, it puts everyone on notice and high alert. Anyone close by will experience heightened anxiety levels too. Now the interesting part is that you and I can calm down from that situation by going somewhere quieter, having a cup of tea, or even going outside for a walk. But where does the person with dementia go? Where can they go and who will help them get there? Often the only option available to them is to escalate or to be managed. This is why change is so essential.

Sorry seems to be the hardest word

I believe that the words, 'I'm sorry' are the most under-utilised words within this industry. There's a perception by many that by saying 'I'm sorry' they're expressing an admission of guilt. If you are in the wrong, there's nothing more defusing than recognising it yourself. Saying you're sorry can be said in a context that has the ability to build bridges. It says to the receiver, I'm extending my hand to you because 'I am sorry you aren't happy' or 'I'm sorry you're hurting.' Those simple words can have an impact that many other words can't even come close to matching.

When someone in a shop dismisses a query by saying, 'No, we don't have it', we're often left feeling deflated. The person made it clear that they didn't care, and they bluntly told us so. In contrast, there's the shop assistant who might say something along the lines of, 'I'm sorry we don't have that in stock. Would you like me to see if I can find it elsewhere?'. The words ultimately have the same meaning, but we are left feeling more of a connection with them. In that moment they leave us feeling like they care. At the end of the day, it wasn't their fault that the item wasn't in stock, but they're still going to try to help you get it sorted.

That's how we connect with others. By saying 'I'm sorry,' it changes and reframes our thinking. It reassures the other person that although we may not be able to fix what's broken, we are there offering support regardless. And it saddens me when occasionally staff will say that they refuse to apologise to someone with dementia when they clearly haven't done anything wrong. I can see a behaviour brewing from the other side of the room, and I can tell you it's not from the person with dementia.

Behaviours

What's interesting with behaviours is that they're something that all of us have. What is surprising is that we focus on behaviours in those with dementia but make excuses for those without dementia. To think that behaviours are the exclusive result of dementia leaves many thinking there really isn't much that can be done but to manage them. The following definition for behaviour mentions nothing about having dementia or cognitive decline as a pre-cursor for a person to experience it.

The response of an individual, group, or species to its environment – Merriam-Webster Dictionary

We all go through our everyday lives with needs and wants to be filled. We spend our days seeking out ways to satisfy those needs at every opportunity. If I'm thirsty or hungry, I'll likely head straight to the tap or the fridge. If I'm out and about I'll stop at a shop. If I'm cold, I'll turn on the heating. If I'm short of money, I'll just pop into the bank. If I miss someone that I haven't spoken to in a while, I'll just use my phone to call them. If a need or want can't be satisfied, we're often left feeling sad or annoyed. It's annoying when there is no coffee or milk left or when someone else has eaten the last cream filled donut. What if I needed to speak to someone but discovered my phone was flat? We may have the ability to hide or cover our disappointment or we may also choose to make it known to the world. Especially if it involves coffee!

The story is no different for someone with advancing dementia. They go through each day with the same types of needs and wants but in most cases are unable to express them.

They are often unable to meet their own needs and wants due to a lack of opportunity or ability. But what we do see instead, is often an expression of that need, which is often very quickly labelled as a 'behaviour.' This form of expression may be the only avenue that the person has left to try and let those around them know that they're sad, disappointed, frustrated or maybe even scared.

When we say that someone with dementia can no longer communicate, we couldn't be further from the truth. There may not be the verbal responses that are delivered in a way that we're used to, but often the messages are very clear. What the person needs from me is to just keep trying to decipher those messages; to develop tools and strategies that will support them to get those messages across. This isn't always easy, but the best part is that it's not always impossible. All that I need to do is to stop expecting them to meet me halfway and to do more to meet them where they are at.

Red, blue, yellow, and green flags

The red flags are always there, right from the start. Flags are the person's only way to signal to us that something's not right in their world or that they need or want something. Unfortunately, in the world of dementia, the red flags often come in a variety of colours, which means they're not always easy to identify. It's the blue, yellow and green ones that may signify changes are happening but may be overlooked. But if we look closely enough, it's not uncommon to see these flags before they've even been raised.

Gladys had her favourite chair in the dining room, the spot where she liked to sit for meals. If Gladys didn't get her seat, she became distressed and started yelling. That chair was important to her routine. We knew that mealtime was close, and that Gladys was on her way down the corridor. It was at that moment that we noticed another resident, Roger, sitting in her chair. We had a choice to make. Roger was there first so I could just explain to Gladys that she missed out today, but she could sit in that seat next time. Roger wasn't fussed where he sat, so the likely scenario was to do everything possible to get Roger to move to another seat before Gladys got there. By taking that pre-emptive action, it alleviated distress for everyone involved.

That is an example of a red flag that hadn't even been taken out of its bag. It was kept tucked away safely so that it didn't need to be used. These are the moments that staff anticipate all the time and do an amazing job in keeping things calm. It's when the flag comes in a different colour or doesn't look as obvious, that things slip through the net and then matters take a turn for the worse.

With dementia, the warning flags can be any colour. We know when we see a red flag what that means. It's the subtle signs or flags that get missed that could hold the key to de-escalating or diffusing a situation earlier.

Noise

It is not always understood that someone living with advancing dementia is likely to struggle to process more than one sound at a time. For someone to stand a chance at understanding what is being said there shouldn't be any competing sounds. Take a moment to think of the environments that you've been in. What noises are you likely to hear? Through my own experience they include things like televisions, music, building works, voices, phones, call bells, trolleys, banging doors, air conditioners, cutlery, plates, pots, pans, PA systems and the list goes on.

Do we set people up for the best possible chance of hearing what's being said to them? Or do we just yell a little louder over the top of any background noise? How do you think all of this combined noise impacts on someone's agitation levels? What we do know is that throughout the day, anxiety levels are on the rise, and is that any surprise? If we want to maximise the chances of hearing success, we all need to be more aware and responsible for the sounds that surround a person. Some of those sounds may be difficult to modify, but awareness on our part means we can at least turn off the things that are within our reach. It may be as simple as turning off the television or music rather that talking over the top of it, that can make all the difference.

Show me the way to navigate my day

All of us are reliant on cues to get us through our day. There are cues that guide us as to what we'll do or experience next. A usual day might start with an alarm clock to say it's time to get up. Hunger then kicks in, so it's time for breakfast. A glance at the clock indicates that it's time to head to work. The traffic lights warn of the need to stop and wait for others. A diary tells me what the workday will look like, where meetings will be held and at what time. It also shows those personal appointments, so they don't get missed along the way. The sun starts to set, showing that the day is coming to a close and that sleep time is near.

Cues are happening all day every day. Think about what it would be like to take away cues from our day or if we lost the ability to interpret them. There would likely be a lot of chaos, frustration, and many missed events. Even the position of the sun can give us a rough indication of whether it's morning, afternoon or that evening is approaching. Cues point us in the right direction, and they influence how we feel and how things are going to unfold for us.

If an alarm is missed, anxiety levels go up. When cues don't present themselves to us, we are left floundering. Think about getting off a plane at an international airport and finding they don't have any signage, knowing that you'll need to just wander aimlessly until you find where you think you're meant to be.

Cues are so much a part of our daily routine that we may not notice they're even there, but we certainly notice them when they're not. Think of the everyday experience for someone living with dementia. What cues are there to guide them? Are those cues ones they can connect and relate to?

I went to see a movie with my family. We settled into our seats with drinks and popcorn and waited for the movie to start. We sat through the advertisements and movie trailers, all while the house lights were dimmed, as they usually are. We all know that when the main movie comes on, the house lights go off altogether. We continued watching, but I suddenly became confused. I wasn't sure whether the movie we were there to see had just started. I questioned this in my mind because it looked like it could be our movie, but the house lights were still on.

I've been pre-programmed over many years to know that house lights go off and that cues me that my movie has started. I hadn't seen any key characters so self-doubt kicked in and I thought it must just be another trailer. But the trailer went on and on. I started to think that this could in fact be our movie, but I couldn't settle into it because all I could focus on was the lights that were still on.

So, what did I do? I leant across my young son and in a loud whisper said to my husband, 'The house lights are still on!' To which he replied, 'Well, yeah.' I sat back in my seat, but I couldn't relax. Things were just not as they should have been. In the big scheme of things, it really was not a big deal, but I just couldn't let go of the feeling that things just weren't right. This just isn't what happens. Again, I leant across to my husband and in a loud whisper said, 'The house lights are still on.'

I clearly read my husband's facial expression and without any words, I could see what he was thinking, 'What do you want me to do about it?' I slumped back into my seat feeling defeated but then it happened. I noticed someone going down the steps. Suddenly with the flick of a switch, the house lights went off and I could relax into the movie.

Yes, I'm the first to admit that this is a trivial story with no real consequence. But that one small cue that should have been there wasn't, and it had the potential to change my whole experience. The experience had started to impact on my behaviour. If I had lacked a filter or coping mechanism for my anxiety, the whole cinema may have been aware of my situation.

This example ticks so many boxes - communication, cues and behaviour - and they all belonged to me. Sometimes it's the smallest things that can throw us out of sorts. When you're supporting someone with dementia, look further than the big things that might be causing confusion because quite often it's the little things that can have the biggest impact.

No way, I'm not doing it

I've had many staff say over the years that if they were to end up in care one day, that they wouldn't tolerate or put up with what currently goes on within the system. They tell me that they know their rights and they will speak out about the wrongs that they see. They firmly say that they won't be ordered around by staff.

My reply to this statement has always remained constant. I tell them that if they're planning some sort of coup, to influence or make changes to the system, not to wait. I advise them to take whatever action they think would be productive and to do it now, do it today. The thing is, if they put if off until tomorrow and end up in care, their voices become null and void because once you have dementia and are in care, your voice is no longer as influential as it once was.

Why can't we see that's what people living with dementia are already doing on a daily basis? Many are often just trying to exercise their rights or to just be heard, requests that are often labelled as a behaviour and so fall on deaf ears. I say to those planning to stand up to the system to not leave their run too late. Because if you do, the system may have to find you a higher dose of sedation and stronger restraints. The rules unfortunately, aren't always the same. We have the opportunity to change the system today. You are a part of that change as much as I am. That's why we're on this journey together.

Who's in charge here?

When reviewing the behaviours of a person within a training group, I'll often ask them who they think holds the weight of power in the working environment. There will commonly be those that will say without justification that it's the person with dementia. I'm shocked every time I hear this response. I feel it's then so important to reframe this perspective so that we can destigmatise it. When the person's extreme behaviours are seen, it's often because the red flags weren't noticed or dealt with early enough leaving all those involved feeling unnerved or even frightened.

While I totally understand the response, it saddens me that the shift in thinking occurs because the scared, frightened, or frustrated individual has reached breaking point. No one understands or sees the emotional or physical pain that the person with dementia is in. This highlights the need to again explore further who the person living with advancing dementia is. They are someone with a disease of the brain who finds themselves in permanent long-term care. They have no possible chance of regaining and resuming their former life. Yet the perception is that they have the upper hand, that it's them that holds the power over someone who freely makes decisions with their own life. It's not the person with dementia who gets to leave at the end of the shift and go home. They are not the person with power.

Carmella's story …

I reflect back to a job I was tasked to during my ambulance days, one that ended with one of the biggest lightbulb moments I've ever had. I was nearing the end of a long 12-hour day shift. I'd told my partner that I was heading out that evening and that I really hoped we'd finish on time. Half an hour before knocking off, we were dispatched to a job that meant there was no way we would finish on time. I felt tired and deflated. The worst part for me was that it wasn't even a high enough priority to use lights and sirens.

We arrived at a care home and met a lovely Italian woman named Carmella. She was unwell and needed to go to hospital. I checked her over and although she was unwell, she wasn't in need of any urgent medical attention. I thought to myself, if we keep things moving, I might still salvage some of my evening.

I was dedicated enough to my job to not even consider compromising care. But what I could do was keep things moving. Unfortunately, Carmella was in a difficult area to access so staff had offered to walk her out to the stretcher. Carmella was mobile but she walked very slowly. There was nothing I could do to help as staff slowly assisted her towards the stretcher. So, although I knew I couldn't speed things up at that moment, as soon as she was on the stretcher we could get going.

She arrived at the stretcher and in the blink of an eye we had her safely tucked up on the stretcher with seatbelts on. A final check of her observations and we were on our way. We took off through the corridors and commenced winding back to the front door. Now Carmella didn't speak or understand English, so I made sure that I was giving her reassuring smiles and touches to her arm. I told her she was OK.

We reached the front door and then realised we didn't have a code for the door keypad. We faced another delay. But I continued to offer Carmella my caring and reassuring smile along with gentle touches to her arm. We waited until a staff member eventually arrived to help us with the code and it was then that Carmella started saying something in Italian. I called the staff member back and asked if she spoke Italian and whether she could tell me what Carmella was saying.

It was in that moment that I just stopped and felt like I had been punched in the stomach. The staff member said that Carmella was asking if she was dying. I instantly responded with, 'Dying? No, tell her she's not dying,' and I started shaking my head to her. I asked the staff member whether she knew why Carmella would say that, why she thought she was dying? She replied that Carmella had thought that because we were rushing it must mean she was dying.

I just stopped and felt so saddened. I couldn't believe I had left someone feeling like that. I knew I hadn't compromised her care in anyway. I knew I'd been nice. I'd been friendly, and I'd continued to show care and compassion. But what I missed was a major detail that inadvertently drove up someone else's stress levels. I missed the fact that because I believed I was communicating effectively with Carmella, that she was receiving and interpreting the intended messages.

I realised in that moment that because we didn't share a common language, Carmella was limited in the information she had for making sense of what was going on. All she really had was the body language and actions of those around her. I knew that I'd never make that same mistake again. And to this day, that story is still clearly etched in my memory. I remember it as if it happened yesterday, but if you ask me where I was heading that night? I have no idea.

Question for reflection …

How do negative or disinterested people in your world impact on you? Do they impact on how you feel or how you're likely to respond?

The gift …

We all have the ability to make more of a difference than we think we are capable of. It often comes down to investment of time and a little creative thinking.

'It's not that we don't hear you, but we don't always understand what you mean.'

• Care home resident •

8 • Adjusting and reframing our thinking

'Depending on their position and status, health professionals may lack the channels of influence to implement new practices.'

- L. Phillipson, B. Goodenough, S. Reis, R. Fleming, p. 78

A new dialogue is needed to move forward in the care of people with dementia. It's about us going about things differently so that we can influence the next generation of support providers coming our way, caring individuals who may one day be responsible for our care. We are still at the beginning of being the change dementia care needs. By changing the conversation and reframing our thought processes and dialogue, we take a step in the direction we need to head. While there are processes in place for everything to do with clinical and personal care, how we tackle everything else is done in a much more ad hoc fashion. It's time to reframe our thinking about how we'll better incorporate personal accountability for all the areas that formalised procedures don't include.

No longer about just turning up

There is no doubt there are systemic issues that are far bigger than us to be dealt with to change dementia care. While these should be acknowledged, our focus is solely on the things that you and I can influence. Our focus is on how we 'turn up' each day, what we bring when we enter the door of someone living with dementia. Can we add any real value to the life they now live? If I'm having a bad day, chances are good that I'll rub off on others I meet throughout the day. I'll share my bad day vibe, a vibe and attitude that has the ability to spread misery far and wide. This doesn't make me a bad person, but it means I need to be in tune to the damage I can inadvertently cause. I need to be honest with myself about how I'm feeling and how that may come across and impact others. I need to ask myself frankly whether I really should be at work that day. This is also about having better conversations for supporting our fellow co-workers by being aware of what I currently do when I see a co-worker struggling and knowing how I can support them while still getting my own job done.

What we need to do

As I've said, I don't profess to know what it's like to have dementia, but I think it's important to have the conversation. If we don't talk and have discussions about what it might be like, how can we change, and better tailor our services? By moving our thinking and changing our understanding, we can start to have and share in many more lightbulb moments. By bringing to life the unspoken words that those living with dementia already share with us, we place ourselves in a better position to hear their stories. We're better placed to reflect when we try our best to connect with others and our one size fits all approach doesn't appear to work. We create a solid base for our own ongoing self-evaluation and self-discovery. With our own personal systems in place, we build a confidence within ourselves from which we can seek guidance from others both internally and externally. We can more meaningfully contribute to the creation of a team-based approach.

We hold the balance of power. We are the ones who can influence how a day for someone with dementia might look. We have the ability to take a step back and think how uncomfortable we'd feel sitting in that same chair all day. I've no doubt in my mind that the frustrations we feel in this area don't even come close to those experienced by the person, a frustration they would desperately want us to see and understand. How much we over complicate the simple things!

We stand before the person with a textbook trying to work out what's wrong with them, having our invisible bookmark firmly placed in the chapter on behaviours without realising that if we just turn over a few pages, there's a chapter on just listening. When we listen, we are more open to that which is being told or shared with us. Our eyes and ears are opened, and we can see and hear without analysis or judgement. We reflect concern for the needs of another human being. Keep the starting point simple and if that doesn't work, then try something different. If that doesn't work, then mix things up again. If things still don't seem to make a difference then sure, go get your invisible textbook. But don't just get stuck on the behavioural chapter.

It's all in the response

Our reactions and responses are pivotal to how everyday exchanges with another human being will end up panning out. They can influence whether everyone gets frustrated and gives up trying or whether they keep trying to find a different and better way to connect. Unfortunately, there is no one size fits all approach to connecting with another person and therein lies the problem. When we attempt to connect with someone there are so many hidden variables.

Difficulties with communication and connection are widespread and not just reserved for dementia but for some reason we've been conditioned to think they are. It's important that we don't just hear what people with dementia are trying to say but to provide them with the opportunity to speak. How can we create better opportunities? How can we start the dialogue? Consider thanking a person with dementia for something they do or share with you no matter how big or small it may appear. Thank them for helping you to complete a task. Practise being grateful more openly that you know them and what they have to contribute.

I remember spending time in a care home and observing the running of a shift. I was blown away when afternoon handover commenced, and I got to share in and witness something that warmed my heart. Within the nurses' station there was a round table with seats all around it, obviously set up for meetings. At handover time, all the afternoon staff filed in but then I noticed that residents were filing in too. It got quite crowded, but no one seemed to mind. It wasn't just staff who sat at the table but also a small number of residents who had previously worked in clinical roles. The staff who didn't get a seat just stood behind and leant on desks. I couldn't believe it and I could do nothing but smile. These were residents with dementia, residents who had limited capacity to retain or spread the confidential information they were sharing in. The conversations were happening so fast that I doubt anyone would have heard the words being spoken. One lady even dozed off. The important part for them was not in the sharing of top-secret information, but the fact that they were being included. Their former professional roles were recognised, and they were part of the team. This is a great example of uncomplicated dementia care.

I have been so fortunate to have had the opportunity to work within a diverse range of settings, that have enabled me to see and support people living with dementia from a myriad of angles. I've been privileged to share in different perspectives of a person's life not just in the latter stages but throughout their whole progression of dementia. It gave me a unique insight into their world, and I will be forever grateful for the stories and insights that have been shared along the way.

Perhaps you've had the same experience, perhaps not. You may have informal training you have received and not even realised it. It may have been through the support that you have given or are providing to a parent, grandparent, friend, neighbour or someone within your community. Those lightbulb moments and gifts that they offer are those that we must capture and bring to the forefront.

I admit that sometimes I feel like a fraud in the work I do. There are those that at times hang on my words like I'm sharing a scientific breakthrough, but I'll never forget a comment made during a training session on communication I delivered once for hospital staff. Following the session someone put up their hand and with a quizzical look asked, 'But, isn't this how we should be treating everybody?' And in that moment, I was gladly exposed. That person had a lightbulb moment and willingly shared it with the rest of the auditorium. Who would have thought that through teaching others about the complexities of dementia that the take home message would be how to be nice to another human being? The rules are most certainly the same and, in that moment, it reminded me that we all need to do a self-check every now and then to ensure that we're meeting the mark.

But they said it couldn't be done

Our starting point for connecting with someone is often more complicated than it really needs to be. In an area influenced so heavily by clinical practice, I think it's important to never underestimate the value of going back to the basics. Simplifying approach and conversation is such a great place to start. If we don't use that as our starting point, and go straight to complex strategies and solutions, we're often left feeling like we've run out of options with nowhere else to go.

I feel very fortunate to have started nursing so many years ago in a time before risk assessments and work-place safety. While these policies are vitally important and needed to be implemented for the safety of all, when they came into practice, they left the interpretation of risk wide open. I had been fortunate to have witnessed firsthand and had the opportunity to engage in and encourage meaningful engagement for residents within the care setting. To see the joy for someone in contributing to their own meaningful existence was wonderful. But seemingly overnight, due to fear of liability, opportunities in many cases abruptly shut down completely. Residents who had actively participated in kitchen duties were no longer permitted to enter the kitchen. With no transition in place for modifying the tasks residents were doing or finding somewhere safer for them to be done, everything came to a grinding halt.

Adjusting expectations

A positive step forward over the years has been the increasing practice of interpretation of policies to hear staff proudly say, 'Things can be done differently, we already do it. We try to balance the risk with quality of life.' An example of this is the idea of everyone needing to be woken up early and ready by a specific time as compared to a care home where residents can get up when they please.

Moving forward, we need to create a framework within which people can reflect on new concepts being trialled and bring them to life in current practice. We need a framework that enables staff to take a step back and reflect on situations as they evolve around them, to feel safe enough to ask whether they, in some way, contributed to what might have happened to the person with dementia. They need to be supported in such a way that they can reframe their thinking and learn from the experience and to share with others when they find a better or easier way.

Staff need to be better supported to positively influence times where staff numbers and resources may not be freely available. Staff should be enabled to be creative with their caring and be part of the creation of a new model of care where things can be done efficiently but in a more streamlined way. Staff continue to believe the repeated narrative that the lack of staffing numbers and available resources are the reasons for the limitations faced when providing care to someone with dementia. While these are certainly major factors, they aren't the whole story. We can shift the focus on that which we can change and work forward from there.

We need to make time to pause and reflect on our own practice within the working environment, a time where staff can provide productive feedback and receive feedback accordingly and see the bigger picture that we're a part of. If what I'm doing is impacting negatively on another human being, as much as that may hurt, I would want to know. I would want to change what I'm doing or be shown a better or different way so I can have a positive impact. That is, after all, why we all signed up to care for others in the first place.

As Pie in the Sky as this may sound, it can be realistically achievable if everyone is on board, is committed to the job at hand and feels comfortable having the frank discussions based on relationships between colleagues that include trust and common goals for improved care. When we can challenge each other in a safe environment it often opens dialogue that's never been had before. It starts conversations for a better tomorrow.

I remember conducting a session with some residential staff who were trusting enough to engage and connect with the process I was offering them - so much so, that before I even had the chance to pack up my gear, there was a group of five staff who went straight to the manager who did the session with them. They told her they were ready for change and that they wanted to be a part of it. This was five staff out of the twenty in attendance. Five staff with a palpable passion to do more. Five staff who knew that together they could make a real impact.

The other fifteen left straight away. Maybe someone needed to catch a bus. Maybe someone needing to pick up their kids. Just because they left quickly doesn't mean they wouldn't support those that were choosing to take a stand. Some of the fifteen might also have been the disgruntled workers who had been around for so long and had given up on change long ago. Maybe this could offer them a beacon of hope to get back on board. And lastly, of the fifteen that just up and left, there might be those who don't give a toss. They took the job for the money and couldn't be bothered to find anything else. They're the ones that make the job harder for everyone else and they're the ones that can ensure that someone with dementia has an average day. If everyone steps up for change, these are staff that will quickly be exposed.

Not everyone has to or will get onboard with a change in thinking. It only takes a few to commit and others will follow. So many staff are out there just waiting for a natural leader to emerge among the ranks, not one that will take charge and tell everyone what to do, but a leader who will be the voice that will inspire others to naturally follow. The old saying 'practice what you preach' rates a mention here. It is being and showing others a better way that will ultimately lead to changes big and small. The group of five were brainstorming with the manager before I'd zipped up my bag. They were discussing ideas for things they should trial and whether they could meet as a workplace dementia action group. It was wonderful to witness and I was grateful that their manager was someone they felt they could approach and trust with their ideas and passion. On reflection, all I did was start the conversation. The staff were willing to do the rest.

It is so important to create opportunities for sharing information and brainstorming ideas for change. Being creative with care is just as important, and at times, just as valuable as whether someone used their bowels or had all their medications. There are new benchmarks in town with a meaningful life belonging right up there.

Adjusting my own expectation

I don't profess to be a Dementia Expert or a Dementia Whisperer or any of the variants I've heard over the years. If you want to give me a title, the one I would feel most comfortable with is a Dementia Information Seeker. I am constantly on the lookout for new learning opportunities for myself that I can then share with others. My learning in this area has been influenced not only by researchers but equally by the person with dementia, families and the staff I get the privilege to work with along the way. The greatest lesson for me was in accepting that it was me who needed to change, to be open to the concept that it was me who needed to think differently. Adapting the way I thought and practised would be the only way

I could offer the greatest level of support and service that those with dementia needed from me.

I could see that the person living with dementia was incapable of changing the way they responded when challenges came their way. Their daily struggle and energy were already consumed with the difficulties that this destructive disease presented them with. They were doing their best to try to navigate the obstacles that dementia put in their way. They were already doing more than enough. It was unreasonable of me to add to their burden by expecting them to be something they couldn't.

I learnt to never blame the person. And they in turn taught me to focus on what they could do and to do so without trying to manage or control. I realised that it had never really made sense to me to do that in the first place. I learnt to reframe my questions from, 'How do I fix, manage or make them do?' to, 'What does this person need from me?' The answers are very different and will always provide me with something much more tangible to work with. What many have needed from me was a sense of normality. They needed me to restore calmness when the chaos became all too consuming. Dementia had robbed them of the ability to do so for themselves, but it hadn't impacted me. I still had the ability to think for us both.

Thinking differently

The moment we take ownership of the mistakes and situations we've unknowingly contributed to, is the moment we begin to truly hear the cries for help that were right in front of us all along. From that moment, we'll better serve those who need it most. And we won't do it by working harder as an individual but by coming together to share our insights and our learnings. Dementia education, along with technology and research, is now taking us further in leaps and bounds. But that's of no use if we don't do anything useful or meaningful with the information it all provides. We can only serve those impacted by dementia better by coming together in a way we've never done before. Are you the dementia difference? Are you prepared to be a voice for those without?

Mavis' story ...

Mavis had dedicated her whole life to dutifully look after her family and keeping the home fires burning. She took pride in her home skills and you could see the meaning and a feeling of contribution they gave her. On a late shift, Mavis could be seen wandering aimlessly around the care home looking lost. Many residents had already gone to bed and she had lost her daytime cues for where she should be heading and what she should be doing next. The beautiful thing about Mavis was that she just wanted to be part of the team. She wanted to help where she could do her bit. I have no doubt that this brought her a sense of comfort and connection not only to her environment but also to those around her.

If I, or my colleagues, saw Mavis and if we were on supper duty, we'd take her along for the ride. She would hand out biscuits or sandwiches and would come into the kitchen and dry the cups and dishes as we washed them. These moments would give us a quiet opportunity to chat with her and reflect on times gone by. In the peace and quiet of that moment, Mavis would initiate conversation which was something she looked too overwhelmed to do during the day. Many of her stories had a beginning and many never had an end and some were even missing bits in between but to see her tea towel in hand, drying a cup with a relaxed look on her face and a cheeky smile was something I will always remember.

These are the opportunities that we need to give back. There are many staff out there learning to think outside the square and give back what has been lost for so long. We continue asking the question, 'Can we do better for those in our care?' There are still those who work firmly from within the box and fear the consequences of risk. Working within the guidelines is so important but it's also vital that we share our learnings with each other so that there is a more consistent approach to dementia care not just within a specific care home but also across the board.

Question for reflection …

What is one thing you could change about yourself today that would have a positive impact for someone living with dementia? (Hint: Ensure it is a small change and realistic in nature)

The gift …

Acknowledging and accepting that it's me who needs to change better places me for greater service. To expect someone who is experiencing insurmountable challenges in their life to change and fit in with me is unrealistic in expectation. But if I'm the one to change, then the possibilities for a better life are endless.

Changing me and adjusting my mindset will ultimately lead to far better outcomes.

'I wish I could do more for the person I'm caring for …'

• Care staff •

9 • Looking through the portal to a better future

'Care is enhanced through breaking down barriers between teams, placing the person with dementia at the centre of care, educating care providers and ensuring sensitivity to local context.'

- L. Jones, B. Candy, S. Davis, M. Elliott, A. Gola, J. Harrington, N. Kupeli, K. Lord, K. Moore, S. Scott, V. Vickerstaff, R. Omar, M. King, G. Leavey, I. Nazareth & E. Sampson, p. 15

Where are we heading?

What do we ultimately want change to look like? Are our expectations realistic? Are we continuing to think too small? My belief is that we all know what good and supported holistic care should look like for someone with dementia. But is the vision big enough and what's holding us back from creating it? Holistic dementia care will steer us in the direction of never-before-seen change. Imagine a future dementia world that kicks all the ultimate care goals:

- Minimised hospitalisation rates for both short and long term admissions. (We know that only increases the anxiety and agitation levels of someone with dementia.)

- More independent and supported living arrangements earlier.

- Assisting families and staff to have a greater understanding of the term active treatment and how it compares to comfort care.

- Early development of and discussions around advanced care directives by everyone involved.

- Early implementation of a palliative approach.

- Tailored end-of-life practices to better support the person.

What else could we see?

We can be better in the dementia care space by honouring the stories of those who have passed through our lives and those we have worked alongside, bottling up their messages and teachings for continuous improvement. Where are those lessons currently kept? Where are the amazing stories and lessons that those with dementia, their families, and staff have shared along the way? The sad truth is that they may have been shared with one, two, maybe twenty people but then they slipped away. They were lost when the person left the industry or this world. Valuable resources and learning tools now gone.

Our goal is to better capture those stories and learnings and treat them as the true gold that they are. These stories will ultimately raise the profile of the 'nice to have' stuff and turn it into the 'need to have' stuff. The problem we face is identifying the messages those stories have to offer.

I want to share a quote from Ellen, a beautiful lady I worked alongside over 25 years ago. Ellen had a saying that she would always say on repeat. She would say it whenever care was provided to her or when you said hello to her in passing. Morning, noon, and night the words that she would share were always the same. She was a lady who was able bodied but who knew that her mind was letting her down. Her gratitude for any care provided to her was humbling. She had sad eyes with a look of despair and she always looked lost. She felt frustrated, never knowing where she was supposed to be. But multiple times a day she would force a smile and say, 'Laugh and the world laughs with you, cry and you cry alone.' For someone living with dementia, her message to the world couldn't have been clearer. The saddest part was not realising there was so much more we could have done.

The time for change was yesterday

The time for change is now! Once we make a start, we will never be able to look back. There are mountains to be moved and we do this best together. I speak for many amazing people out there who have said, 'I'm tired of trying to move the mountains on my own.' Many skilled individuals have left the aged care industry not because they didn't care but because they were sick of not having the opportunity to practise dementia care from the heart, to practise in a way they knew deep down they were great at. They were weighed down by the politics, the system and by those who habitually said there was no money.

These were our peers and they just wanted to do more than their job. They left because they didn't feel they could make a difference in a way that they believed really mattered. Everyone working and contributing in this area should feel valued and come together as a true team. How wonderful it would be to create a new world of dementia care where those staff lost over the years saw a door opening through which they could return.

It's up to us to put a value on dementia care. It's priceless. I have been fortunate to see many care homes where things are progressing and changing for the better. It excites me that the momentum has started. But my concerns still sit with the limitations that exist, that initiatives can still only go so far before a full stop is put in place. We must continue to challenge the system to keep doing it better.

Everyday moments of insight

Our future in dementia care must involve and incorporate our learnings but it must also include our strengths, the gifts we all hold. We need to think about what we already have right in front of us that remains unutilised. What do we already hold in our hands? We are all trained to deliver a standard of care but by helping to draw out the unique qualities of staff we will develop areas of care that remain untapped. Our future includes understanding who we are and taking responsibility for our actions. Some of my own personal insights that could impact on my practice include:

- I've got a loud voice – not useful when people are napping or sleeping.

- My loud voice can be used for either good or for evil.

- I'm the one ultimately responsible for the actions I choose to take.

- I'm ultimately responsible for how I respond to any situation.

- Change can come if I do my part – I can't change a whole system, but just do my part.

- I accept that I cannot be everything to everybody.

- I must combine my talents with the talents of others if I want to make others take notice.

- I can be a strong voice for those without and accept the responsibility that carries.

- When I bring together not just the skills and knowledge of amazing people but also their passion and compassion, the sky is the limit for what can ultimately be achieved.

I've met so many staff over the years who have not understood or been unable to grasp the value of this concept. But I've also met so many staff who have understood this even if it's not on a conscious level. They are the staff whom I have been fortunate to watch not working to a script but providing care instinctively and intuitively. They know the person, they know some of their story, they know what makes them tick. They know what a specific person needs without them uttering a word.

This isn't a skill they were taught in a classroom and it wasn't something that someone else told them to do. It was something that felt right and so they did it more. This form of practice cannot be seen or documented. And because it doesn't appear at face value to provide any consistency of practice, these intuitive and instinctive skills and knowledge are not valued or replicated in anyway. But this is a form of practice that we need to take more seriously because it often uncovers the answers that so many of us are likely to be seeking. If only we could capture that which is there for the taking and put it on display for all to benefit from.

Going back to basics

That instinctive need to offer care and support is evident within the many staff I have worked with. What I have noted is that it's a trait that isn't limited to the work environment. The intuitive nature of what staff do, means these instinctive practices are often occurring regardless of whether they are working on a shift or out within their local community. It is an unacknowledged skill that kicks into action whenever they see someone floundering or lost out in public.

Some years ago, I was living within a regional area and driving home one cold winter's night. It was 9.30pm and no one was around. Because of this, I noticed a well-dressed older man out walking along the footpath and something about him caught my attention. It was late, dark, cold and he didn't appear dressed for a casual walk. Although he walked with confidence, he seemed to lack purpose. Something within me made me turn back to see where he was heading. As he approached a main intersection, I watched him press the button for the lights. He waited, they changed, and he safely crossed. I then watched him press the button for the next light, wait and cross again. All seemed like he knew where he was going until he pressed the next button for the next light, waited and crossed again. One more button press, and he would have gone the full square. I watched with a sense of trepidation. If he completed the circuit, I knew I needed to act, and he did. He calmly pressed the final button, completed the intersection and headed off in a different direction.

I wasn't sure what to do but chose to drive and park ahead of him. I walked back along the footpath towards him as though I too was out for a casual evening walk. I said hello to him, and he responded with, 'Hello,', but with a nervous laugh. I asked him where he was heading on such a cold night and he said, continuing with a nervous laugh, 'I'm not really sure!' Instinct hadn't let me down and as we conversed, I could see he really had no idea where he was meant to be. I introduced myself and as luck would have it, we were a short walk from the local ambulance station. Fortunately, he agreed to walk with me there.

He was taken to hospital where it was established that he did have dementia and he'd wandered away from the house of a relative who wasn't aware yet that he was missing. When we take a moment to connect with someone with dementia, we are presented with an opportunity to change their course and guide them in the direction they need or want to go. This was a man with dementia living in the community. He didn't need fixing and he didn't need managing. He didn't need or want anyone changing his life in any way. All he needed in that moment was someone to guide and point him in the right direction, to help him get to where he needed to be. My responsibility was to make sure he got to his destination while making him feel as though he was still in control of the steering.

Enjoying the lightbulb moments (also known as a-ha moments)

The unverified definition of a lightbulb moment is that moment where you move across from one seat to the next and you see the world just that little bit differently. What motivates and inspires me is when I experience a lightbulb moment. It's that moment where I almost kick myself and wonder how I never saw what now seems so obvious right before my very eyes. What drives me to do more in this space, is the opportunity to not only have my own lightbulb moments but to also share in the lightbulb moments of others, be they families or staff or even someone living with dementia. I've found it incredibly humbling to perhaps be the push that some needed to shift from one seat to the next. When we allow ourselves to move from our old comfortable and well-worn seat to a new one, we see the world from a whole new angle, a whole new perspective. and unless we allow ourselves the opportunity to do this when supporting someone impacted by dementia, then we deprive ourselves of so many lightbulb moments.

The wonderful thing about lightbulb moments is that they can light up a room and they can be contagious. They can infect others because they too want to experience that fleeting sense of euphoria that someone else just felt. Suddenly you get a snapshot and a glimpse of what could be possible, that after years of conditioning there may be an easier or better way to do something. A lightbulb moment is the realisation that with some small tweaking and coming at something from a slightly different way, the impact on the life of another could be huge. And the best part, it's likely to be something that doesn't cost extra time or energy. It might be just reframing something you already do. The impact though not only has the potential to change a moment for someone but may also make your job a whole lot easier.

Lightbulb moments are designed for sharing; they need to be brought to life and to impact others. I love sharing in the lightbulb moments of others. To share an insight that may help others to experience the same or their own lightbulb moment is such a gift to be embraced. Jenny's story is an example of one of my favourite lightbulb moments I've shared.

When dementia takes away so much, what untapped potential do we hold to give back?

Jenny's story ...

I was working with a group of staff and discussing the potential effects of our actions and the impact they might have on someone with dementia. We talked about how even our most well-intentioned interactions may inadvertently be a negative in disguise. Suddenly, a staff member at the back of the large group, Jenny, put her hands over her mouth. She let out a high-pitched squeal and said, 'Oh no!', and continued on repeat. I stopped to check if she was OK, but she continued to repeat, 'Oh, no!'. She eventually stopped and bravely shared with us that she had just had a lightbulb moment, a moment she reflected on and realised that perhaps with good intention she had likely missed the intended mark.

Now Jenny was someone I had never met before. She had a caring manner and caring voice and I instantly liked her. This is often where I think caring people can sometimes come unstuck. Just because we care and are known for having a caring nature, doesn't always mean we'll get it right. That doesn't always sit well for caring people to think that they have unintentionally upset or offended someone.

But if we truly want to be the best at what we do, we need to own that we are human. Jenny went on to share how when a resident who had previously not been eating well finished a meal, she genuinely felt overjoyed with a sense of accomplishment for them. She then shared with us just how graphic her joy might have looked to the outside world. She described how she would stand by the person, clench her fists, and put them triumphantly into the air. This was accompanied by a loud singing type voice saying, 'Yayyyy, Yayyyy!'

Jenny realised in that moment of reflection, that the person had finished their meal, not run in a marathon. And in that moment, although caring and well-intentioned, she saw the action for what it was. She suddenly realised for herself how that would likely leave someone feeling. She also commented that she knew she needed to change. And the best part was that no one had to tell her. Through the creation of a safe and friendly environment, Jenny not only allowed herself to navigate her own lightbulb moment, but also felt brave enough to share it with the whole group.

Think about it, you've been feeling a bit down or unwell. You haven't been eating much but tonight for the first time in a long time you finish all your dinner. Imagine a friend or family member standing next to you cheering and clapping because you finished your meal. I was excited to have shared in this lightbulb moment with Jenny. When she gave herself permission to shift to another metaphorical chair, her ability to self-reflect on her daily practice went from there. She allowed herself to just go with the flow and the awakening came from within.

Jenny went on to share how mortified she was to think that she was using a condescending tone and treating adults like children. Her honesty made me like her even more because she embraced change and desperately wanted to be a part of it. She didn't just sit there in quiet contemplation about how she could perhaps do things differently. She made a public declaration about how she screwed up but was now going to do things differently.

Those are the staff I love to work with. They're the staff that inspire me to keep going and to continue sharing the stories where I have got it wrong. Staff like Jenny make me feel braver to say out loud what I think needs to be said. This is the power of vulnerability and being vulnerable is just what we need if we want to take that next step. I just want to add that we did discuss how important it was for her to share the moment she'd felt so happy about. There was nothing to stop her from heading to a colleague or to the staff room to share how happy she felt about Mrs Smith finishing her dinner and hopefully now feeling better.

Question for reflection …

If you don't take a stand and influence change then who will?

The gift …

A lightbulb moment can light up a room and change lives for the better.

'I speak with a quiet voice so never thought I sounded condescending. Until one day I told a resident to open up for his medicine and realised I sounded like I was talking to a child.'

* Registered nurse *

10 • Being the hope for a better tomorrow

'Symptom management near the end of life in dementia is often sub-optimal, although symptom burden may be similar to cancer, chronic obstructive pulmonary disease (COPD) or advanced heart failure.'

- L. Jones, B. Candy, S. Davis, M. Elliott, A. Gola, J. Harrington, N. Kupeli, K. Lord, K. Moore, S. Scott, V. Vickerstaff, R. Omar, M. King, G. Leavey, I. Nazareth & E. Sampson, p. *2*

The need for change

I'll be honest with you. Over the years I've grown tired of attending lectures that sounded amazing, brought a new way of thinking and promised so much. Don't get me wrong, these lectures were usually delivered by talented and passionate people, ones that I truly admired. They were lectures that inspired me to want to do more and left me with a sense of hope that I could make a real difference. What disappointed me was that they often didn't come with a next step, the recipe book I needed for converting those learnings and insights into a format that was ready to be picked up for practical application. I realised for others that could be just the same.

I reflected on the lectures and the training sessions that I had delivered over the years. Did I really make a true impact? I knew that I had left my mark, but did I shift the thinking of a group enough to see them march out the door, back into their everyday role saying that they would do things differently? Did they leave with a plan as to how they would do so? While I hope something that I had said had stuck, I would be naïve to think that my words would carry enough weight to tip the balance from what is always expected to trying something new.

My hope was always that I could start the conversation with others and plant seeds for change. I hoped that when choices needed to be made, maybe they might pick B this time instead of the standard A option. It has bugged me for so long, wondering if I could do more to contribute to this space in making a more tangible difference in bridging the existing gap. Could I possibly create something that would allow others to offer more as well? Could I build a platform that not only highlighted the great information already out there but also brought it to life so that others could connect to it more easily.

I knew that I needed to encourage and inspire others to explore and find their special niche so that they could connect with others and allow the practical learning to continue. By having a way to better harness and share the hidden talents within the industry, we could connect and together create something pretty amazing. What surprised me was that I wasn't very far along my path when I started to meet so many people who were feeling the same way. It was then that I knew we needed a way to come together, a way that would unite us all.

While this book started with my learnings, my hope is that it inspires something in you so that you might want to share your stories too. These stories reflect the areas I've been so privileged to work within and the lives I've shared in. Every reflection of someone's story brings a smile to my face due to the moments shared. I hope this in some small way inspires you to do something bigger with what you've learnt too. It would be such a shame for those moments to be wasted. They should be shared and captured in a way that ensures that no one impacted by dementia goes it alone.

I thought that by creating a book full of my stories, it would hopefully result in future editions that included your stories, along with the stories of others - stories that would reflect the wins and the creativity, the learnings, and the connections. I'm no one special in all of this. I'm purely the holder of the stories. I'm a storyteller who has always struggled to keep inspiring and motivating stories to myself. These stories have been shared with me over many years by those who have lived them first-hand and many have included me in some small part. They were entrusted to me, and others just like me, not just so we could hear how tough things were or about how much physical and emotional pain someone was in, but so we would be gifted with a glimpse into a world that many of us can't relate to. They help us to be better at what we do, so that we can grow and stop doing the things that never really made sense or had a functionable purpose; to cease doing those things that inadvertently lead to or exacerbate someone's pain and suffering.

I'm not perfect and I know you're not either. If we can admit this to ourselves, we instantly get to take a deep breath and move the weight of needing to feel like we know it all and that we need to be perfect or to be experts. Instead, we can just listen to and trust the learnings that are being handed to us in a way that at face value may not be clear to see. It's time to expose our vulnerabilities and to show the person living with dementia how much they have to truly teach us. We can turn the tables and give them back an element of self-worth through which we will grow and change the landscape.

Over the years I have been trusted with an insight into a world I could never imagine myself living in. I have been trusted not to judge but to just listen. My focus somewhere along the line then shifted from the person with dementia to those that I served alongside. I felt frustrated by the things that I knew were wrong and for which we had simply become complacent. I could see more clearly the changes that needed to happen, and it saddened me when others said it couldn't be done.

I'd grown tired of feeling sad and disappointed that people in the advanced stages of dementia were still being forgotten and that families still lived disconnected lives, doing their best with such minimal support, information, and guidance. I knew I couldn't continue to do the same thing day after day, trying desperately to inspire change in this area and feeling as if I was getting nowhere. It was like flinging mud against a wall and hoping some or all of it would stick. I hated feeling that I was continuing to let down the very people I would profess to advocate for.

It's no one's fault for where we find ourselves, but it's everyone's responsibility to come up with a new way forward. This just happens to be my time to try something different and I hope it coincides with yours. If I fail, I want to be able to hold my head high and say to myself, 'At least I tried to find a better way.' If I don't succeed, then maybe I'll inspire others to try something different, even if it's just once.

So many people are out there waiting for us and depending on us to at least give something new a try. I don't ever again want to look another person with advancing dementia, or their family members, in the eye and say, 'I wish there was more I could do.' It is such a defeatist statement when there is so much more I could do. I just need to get out there and do it.

Are you the difference that someone with dementia is waiting for?

So how do we move forward and bring everyone together when it hasn't been done before? We start at the beginning and we take one step at a time. But this time we'll do it together. We'll start by moving that great big spotlight off dementia, the disease, and put it right on the person where it belongs. Together we'll give back some of what dementia has taken away.

I'm ending this book with a new beginning. This last chapter is effectively the first chapter of the next book. The experiences I've shared with you have inevitably bought me to this crossroad - a junction in my career where I've found myself reflecting on what's next. What have those moments I've shared with others really meant? Could they possibly come together for a collective purpose?

Over the last six years I've been confronted on a regular basis with a feeling that there's so much more for me to do. Could I possibly make a difference in a space where I saw a gap, a gap where those that reside in it are alone and where others are spending time trying to navigate the mysteries of what is to come and feeling inadequate and lost? These others are the families, the partners, the children who are tired, broken and ready to give up. This is not because they don't care and not because they no longer love. They are in this space because the system forgot about them and said, 'We've got this now. You don't need to worry.' But that's not how it works. Families don't just stop loving or caring and they don't just give up. Even when they're pushed to their limits they still continue to show up. And they do so not because they don't have a life but because this is still their life.

Families want so desperately to stay connected to and contribute to the life of their loved one with dementia. They just don't know how because it's not modelled to them. Who's showing them how to keep showing up? Who's showing them the ropes? Who's teaching them the role they need and want to play? These questions have stuck with me for so many years and I questioned whether it was an area where I may be able to contribute. I loved working with families and wanted to make a difference in their lives no matter how big or small. If I could funnel every ounce of my own learnings into this area and leave with a sense of satisfaction, then maybe this could be it. I have listened to and shared in enough tears from families to honestly say, 'Yes, I could.' And so we find the beginning of a new story, and a new era where it's time to make a difference.

Do you dare share your care?

When you review your own practice, what is it that you bring to the table? This is about taking a moment to define what your motivation is for being a part of dementia care change, to acknowledge the strong need you have to make a difference in the lives of others, especially those more vulnerable within our community.

The work is hard, the recognition isn't always there and the support and opportunity for growth is often sadly lacking. Imagine though, if you, as an individual could contribute in a way that you knew you had made a difference, one that created an opportunity for you to be able to do more. How would you feel, knowing that you provided a missing piece of the puzzle and provided a new model of care, a new way of thinking?

So, what's your niche? What was the first thing that came to mind? I'd love to share in your wins so that we can motivate each other to never give up on those that need us most. Together we'll share our stories and contribute to amazing things. I'm so inspired by the things that others are doing out there within their communities and within supported care environments. I've always just wanted to bottle them up and share all the wins and experiences with the world. I'd love to hear what you're out there contributing to, what your great ideas are. Are they still in the planning phase or are they ones that you've already taken for a test drive? Were they successful or do they need a bit of tweaking? Are they things that you think others could really benefit from?

Coming up with the plan

If you could do things differently, what would that look like? What would you change? How would you go about changing it? What does your ideal world for people living with dementia look like? Could you create it, see it, and feel it?

This book has given us the opportunity to explore deeper and think about the world of dementia care from the outside looking in. We've looked through the windows and seen things that may not sit well for us. We've seen ourselves through that window and have hopefully experienced an awakening that we can do more for those impacted by dementia. By looking honestly at where we've come from, there is a sense of freedom in moving forward. Attitudes about dementia, and how much power we continue to give it, continue to impact not only how we view dementia but also society's view at large. Attitudes make dementia too big a beast to conquer. So, we give up without even trying. But we aren't tied to the past, nor are we obliged to continue doing things just because someone told us ten or twenty years ago that they were the right thing to do. We don't live the same lives as our parents. Hopefully we have learnt from their life experiences and those that walked before them. We can walk a better path because of them, and not because we followed the same one.

Reframing how we view dementia will impact on how we talk about it and what we expect from others. We have seen it for what it really is, and we've been left shocked that we could have been so blindsided. Dementia didn't take everything. In many cases we just gave things away. By looking through a different lens, we now know that the first one was focussed solely on dementia and we forgot about the person. When we realise this and readjust our way of thinking, the new lens provides a much clearer perspective of what the person's world might be like and how they struggle to navigate through it. We realise that when we walk in the shoes of another, they never have to walk alone again.

By walking on a new path, we're finally able to stop spending time, money, energy and a lot of frustration searching for answers that are often more obvious than we realise. The opportunity we will now create for self-reflection is essential for us moving forward as individuals. We're not defined by the roles we've been given, we need to take ownership and be better at recognising the extra qualities we bring. By looking through a different lens we see endless possibilities for how we can further develop those qualities and how to capture them more formally and incorporate them into whatever role we play. It is only then that other paths will open up and opportunities will abound.

Take a moment just to imagine working in a role for which you feel that true sense of purpose and fulfillment, one that you never thought possible. Imagine the look on the faces of those that you support and seeing a sense of hope and contentment rather than one of despair or withdrawal. Are you finally starting to see which piece of the puzzle you are? You may even be starting to see where that piece might fit. This is an exercise that could be done on a regular basis.

The Dementia Doula role

I want to share with you what's next for me. This book was part one of my journey. Over the years it kept bothering me that nothing was happening in the end-of-life care space for those impacted by advancing dementia. I continued to see a one size fits all approach to care. The care that a person was receiving looked exactly like the care they were receiving when they first came through the doors three, four or maybe even seven years ago. I kept asking how the care and the experience for their families had not have evolved in any way? Why was it that the overall care that they received did not incorporate the comfort care practices required in the final stages of life - measures that are commonplace in any other area of palliative care? Why were families still struggling to connect and left grieving all on their own? Why wasn't anyone doing something about it, why wasn't anything changing in this space? Why wasn't anyone doing anything to influence and make that part of care better for all involved? One day it dawned on me that the someone I could be waiting for was me. If something is bothering me for that long, shouldn't I be the one to take that aspect of care that wasn't sitting well for me and just concentrate on that?

I continued over the years to be drawn to the end-of-life space in dementia. I continued to meet people who deserved so much more but for whom the doors were shut. There was no one to even have a simple conversation with about what was to come and the role they would play. I realised then that I was too small a player to make any big changes. What I did know was not to set my vision towards fixing a whole system. I knew I needed to just focus on an element for which I knew I could make a difference. I felt as if I could at least try to start the conversation and to get the ball rolling.

I couldn't see any way round it. I needed to create a whole new role. This role would enable me to bring the voice of the person to life and make connections with them just that little bit easier. So, because the role didn't exist, I created the role for myself. After searching for a title that would be capture the essence of the role, I settled on – Dementia Doula. I soon realised it was a perfect fit for what I wanted to do and for what I needed to contribute. I thought I would have a hard time convincing others in the care industry of the need. When I took the first step and began describing the Dementia Doula role to my peers, I was shocked that they grasped the concept so readily. Some even said they could see it as the perfect future path for them. I could clearly see that there are so many opportunities out there waiting to be created and that it's up to us to get out there and bring them to life.

If you are interested in what we're doing in the Dementia Doula space, then head over to our website www.dementiadoulas.com.au and check out the amazingness that could await you. You'll find out more about this role in 'The Dementia Doula' – our handbook. My point in referencing this is to encourage you to take a step back and identify a need. Without working out where I fit and without the support of my amazing colleagues, I wouldn't be here right now. I wouldn't be making a difference in a way that I knew I needed to do. So, what are you thinking? I'm all ears.

Hope for a better tomorrow

I hope this resource will be somewhat of a conversation starter rather than provide you with all the answers. I hope that it provides the opportunity to start thinking differently, engage your imagination or extend on what you already know. Whatever the case, we all have a responsibility to share our knowledge in a way that mentors and encourages others in their practice. It's time to take a step forward and start the discussion about what needs to change and how we as individuals will commit to making that happen.

The best part is that nothing, absolutely nothing is currently set-in stone. Practices of the past don't need to be repeated. We are perfectly placed right now to re-write dementia care and to do it in a way that will bring hope and value to the lives of so many individuals. The exciting part is that this isn't about creating a whole new test tube way of doing things. It's about capturing the wonderful and amazing things that you're already out there doing. All we need to do is bottle them up and showcase them for all to see and share in.

You see, somewhere along the line we complicated what it is to support someone with dementia. We truly believed that by clinicalising not just the disease part, but all aspects of care, that we were on the right path. It all got thrown into a clinical model of care and it doesn't all fit as neatly as we'd like. It's the other part that you and I get to influence and be a part of, to play an active role in rewriting the chapters of dementia care that focus on personhood and lifestyle, and the way to connect.

We know what truly matters to people and if there are any doubts about that, we'll ask them. We just have to come together, because what you and I bring will make a wave that will show where we've come from and where we're heading next. We need to take things to a whole new level. I'm excited to share that wave with you and I can't wait to see how far it takes us. So, are you in? Are you the dementia difference that those impacted by advancing dementia are waiting for?

Olive's story …

The need for making a difference came from my very first nursing job over 25 years ago. I worked with Olive during her final stages of dementia. We as staff were very task focused and although we provided good personal care, no one ever spent any quality time with her. By quality time, I mean time spent holding her hand, or even just having a conversation. Nobody ever visited and nobody tried to connect with her during her final years or months on this earth. Many years later I discovered who Olive had been in life and it broke my heart. I stood in silence and shed tears for a woman I had cared for but never really knew, tears for a woman whom none of us had realised held her own beautiful life story.

It was about ten years after having nursed Olive. I had moved through a couple of career changes and was one day keen to explore a new neighborhood I'd just moved into. I visited an old National Trust cottage with gardens that opened to the public once a month. I walked through the cottage, exploring all the old rooms, and effectively going back in time. It wasn't a special cottage in any specific way, but it was special in that it captured Australian history and life as it had once been. It was shared through the eyes of the family who had once lived there, a prominent local man, his wife and two daughters. As I walked through the cottage, I came to some photos on the wall with the back story about how the cottage had come into the care of the National Trust.

The two daughters of the family had inherited the cottage and lived together as single women for many, many years. When the time came for the women to move into care, the cottage was donated to the National Trust. They wanted this beautiful time capsule that they had called home to be preserved for future generations. As I read the story, I was shocked and taken aback to read the names of the daughters. Olive's name stood out to me as though surrounded by a neon light. I stood there in front of a photo of a young Olive and tears welled in my eyes. I felt as if I was meeting Olive for the first time, yet it pained me to know we had already met. It saddened me that the Olive that I knew looked nothing like this photo I was seeing for the first time and that hers was a story I had never known. How could this be?

Olive's life story had been taken away with dementia because of her inability to share it. But the story that was thought to be lost was there all along just waiting to be recovered. No one had stood by her side making sure that we, as staff, knew her story. We had no context for the life she had lived. She had not been famous, but she had a story, a story that would have helped me and others to care for her and connect with her in a more holistic way, a story that would have demonstrated to her that someone was listening to the words she was unable to share. This had a real impact on me, I felt that I'd let her down. And if I'd let her down, then I realised in that moment that I had let down many others too. It wasn't because I didn't care, but because I hadn't taken the time to fully learn their stories. People's stories bring back life to those who, through no fault of their own, have been separated from them. It was Olive's story and the many more that followed that ultimately shaped where I eventually needed to head.

Question for reflection ...

If someone stood at a podium and spoke about you and what you had contributed to dementia care, what would you want them to say?

The gift ...

Once you start opening your eyes and seeing things in a new light, it's like a never-ending rabbit hole of information and lightbulb moments.

Many years ago, I challenged a group I was working with. I asked them if it was possible to impact or positively influence a moment in time for someone else. They thought about it and the responses were mixed. I was surprised to hear so many people answer, 'No.' They really couldn't see how they alone could positively impact a moment in someone's life. I took a step back and slowly tried to navigate and convince the group that they held more power than they realised. I needed them to see that they alone had the power to make someone feel happy or make them feel sad.

During the break I sent everyone outside into the garden for a coffee and fresh air before the next part of our session began. As I prepared notes and resources for when the group returned a female participant walked back into the room. She walked up to me, placed a flower from the garden on the desk right in from of me. She smiled, said nothing, and then walked outside again.

She got it and she showed me she got it. Without saying a word, she made me stop what I was doing. Prior to that, I was consumed and focused on my task in that moment. I connected with her and she made me smile. She walked away while I continued to smile as I picked up and instinctively smelt the flower. I had connected with her and she was determined to connect with me. It was a beautiful moment that showed me how important it was not to over complicate what we are ultimately attempting to achieve.

"Staff are wonderful, and I know they do their best, but they just don't get my dad. They just don't have the time ..."

* Family member *

Notes on Sources

1. Why should we bother?

L. de Witt and D. Fortune, *Relationship-Centered Dementia Care: Insights from a Community-Based Culture Change Coalition,* Dementia Vol. 18(3) (2019) 1146–1165

2. Influences of past practices

A. Gawande, *Being Mortal*, (Wellcome Collection 2015) pg. 71

T. Shakespeare, H. Zeilig and P. Mittler, *"Rights in Mind: Thinking Differently About Dementia and Disability,"* Dementia Vol. 18(3) (2019) 1075–1088

3. Who is Dementia and what is it's story?

T. Shakespeare, H. Zeilig and P. Mittler, *"Rights in Mind: Thinking Differently About Dementia and Disability,"* Dementia Vol. 18(3) (2019) 1075–1088

4. Getting to know the real person

M. Keynes and N. Kucirkova, *'It Brings it all Back, all those Good Times; it Makes Me Go Close to Tears'. Creating Digital Personalised Stories with People who have Dementia,* Dementia Vol. 18(3) (2019) 864–881

5. Context

T. Shakespeare, H. Zeilig and P. Mittler, *"Rights in Mind: Thinking Differently About Dementia and Disability,"* Dementia Vol. 18(3) (2019) 1075–1088

6. Working with someone with advancing dementia

Merriam-Webster Dictionary, 22/2/2021, Dictionary, 1/3/2021, https://www.merriam-webster.com/dictionary/apathy

B. Dewar and T. MacBride, *Developing Caring Conversations in care homes: an appreciate inquiry,* Health and Social Care in the Community Vol 25(4) (2017) 1375-1386

7. Communication & behaviours

Merriam-Webster Dictionary, 22/2/2021, Dictionary, 1/3/2021, https://www.merriam-webster.com/dictionary/behavior

E. Smith, M. Broughton, R. Baker, N. Pachana, A. Angwin, M. Humphreys, L. Mitchell, G. Byrne, D. Copland, C. Gallois, D. Hegney and H. Chenery, *Memory and communication support in dementia: research-based strategies for caregivers,* International Psychogeriatrics (2011) 23:2, 256–263

8. Adjusting and reframing our thinking

L. Phillipson, B. Goodenough, S. Reis and R. Fleming, *Applying Knowledge Translation Concepts and Strategies in Dementia Care Education for Health Professionals: Recommendations From a Narrative Literature Review*, JCEHP Vol 36 (1) (2016) 74-81

9. Looking through the portal to a better future

L. Jones, B. Candy, S. Davis, M. Elliott, A. Gola, J. Harrington, N. Kupeli, K. Lord, K. Moore, S. Scott, V. Vickerstaff, R. Omar, M. King, G. Leavey, I. Nazareth and E. Sampson, *Development of a model for integrated care at the end of life in advanced dementia: A whole systems UK-wide approach,*

Palliative Medicine 2015, 1–17

10. Being the hope for a better tomorrow

L. Jones, B. Candy, S. Davis, M. Elliott, A. Gola, J. Harrington, N. Kupeli, K. Lord, K. Moore, S. Scott, V. Vickerstaff, R. Omar, M. King, G. Leavey, I. Nazareth and E. Sampson, *Development of a model for integrated care at the end of life in advanced dementia: A whole systems UK-wide approach,*

Palliative Medicine 2015, 1–17

Acknowledgments

I have so many people to thank for this book finally coming to life. First and foremost are my husband John and son Louis. You both continue to support me on whatever path life takes me down and for that I will always be grateful.

I want to extend a big thank you to Marie. Your unwavering support over many years will always be appreciated. You have never criticised my crazy ideas or told me that something couldn't be done. And to Lorrie, to know you is to know what it's like to have your own personal cheer squad by your side every single day. I am blessed to know you not only in a professional context but also as a friend.

To Robbie, a beautiful woman from whom I continue to draw inspiration. You will always be my driving force for the work I need to do. It is you I think of when it all seems too hard and I feel like giving up. I picture your smile which says to the world that everything is fine on the outside when beneath the surface you have endured more than many could begin to imagine. Please know I do this for you and your beloved husband, for all those I have met along the way and for those that I know are out there showing up as you have done every single day.

I am indebted to the many people who have shared and trusted me with their experiences. Whether they have been frontline staff, specialists, colleagues, family members or someone living with dementia, their insights have been invaluable to my experiences and learnings. To single any one person out would bring with it a fear of excluding someone of equal importance.

www.ingramcontent.com/pod-product-compliance
Lightning Source LLC
Chambersburg PA
CBHW032145020426
42334CB00016B/1236